D1112854

Nothing *Cheap* and Much that is *CHEERFUL*

John Andrew

with a Foreword by
Bishop Michael Marshall

WILLIAM B. EERDMANS PUBLISHING COMPANY
GRAND RAPIDS, MICHIGAN

255 Jefferson Ave. S.E., Grand Rapids, Mich. 49503

Printed in the United States of America

To my wonderful family on Fifth Avenue

Contents

Foreword

THERE is happiness in preaching," wrote Dr. James W. Alexander, professor at Princeton Theological Seminary from 1849 to 1851.

> It may be so performed as to be as dull to the speaker as it is to the hearers: but in favored instances it furnishes the purest and noblest excitements and in these is happiness. Nowhere are experienced, more than in the pulpit, the clear, heavenward soaring of the intellect, the daring flight of imagination, or the sweet agitations of holy passion.

If we strip perhaps a little of its nineteenth-century hyperbole from this statement, we can see that Professor Alexander knew in his bones both the enthusiasm and excitement of the spoken word as a kind of sacrament of gospel personality. Add to such a high doctrine of the Word the Anglican twin emphasis upon the sacraments and worship, and you have an irresistible chemistry for the conversion of souls.

Truly it is that irresistible chemistry which thousands of New Yorkers have experienced in the ministry and witness of Saint Thomas Church Fifth Avenue—and not least under the distinctive leadership of Father John Andrew during his long ministry in that strategic and formative Gothic extravagance at the heart of Manhattan.

And that, frankly, is part of the secret—namely, a ministry with a heart—*largesse du coeur.* In the following pages you will read a selection of sermons. I can promise you they are not dull. They may not be intellectually arresting—though they convey profound insights with a deceptive sense of simplicity and with a facility of prose style. Their strength, I would suggest, is that they come from the heart of a loving pastor with an imagination fired by the Holy Spirit as well as by the spirit of the community he seeks to serve. For John enjoys being a priest—an enjoyment that is contagious. Further, he enjoys living in New York. He delights in that much-neglected art of conversation, always from the heart, with compassion and passionate conviction. He is given to generous hospitality and relishes every opportunity for human encounter. That in a word is the stuff of which good preachers are made. You cannot get it all from a book. It is the recipe for life—the whole of it, expressed through words, gestures, vestures, and postures! A priest and preacher worth his salt will bring all of this to bear in seeking to set hearts on fire with love, compassion, and conviction.

I am glad that in collaboration with Sam Eerdmans (of Eerdmans Publishing Company) we managed to persuade John to send the manuscripts of his sermons for selection and editing. They arrived—boxes and boxes of them: but then I told myself—"he never does things by half!" So there is extravagance in the following pages. But then there is extravagance in the gospel— divine extravagance and generosity. In the following pages you will find all kinds of little gems of insight and observation— the results of persistent curiosity: an eye for the absurd and above all the ability to laugh long and loud at life, with the church, and above all at oneself. You see, humor and orthodoxy belong together: you can be fairly certain that when faces grow long and sentences even longer, you are never very far from heresy. Orthodoxy and encouragement are never cheap, but they are always cheerful.

Such a banquet of words is generously hosted in these pages and reflects the gospel hospitality that has warmed the hearts and converted the lives of countless people over many years who have been able to visit and worship in Saint Thomas Church Fifth Avenue.

It seemed to us that such a feast should be made available to a wider world through the printed word. Inevitably something is lost when you seek to capture the spoken word and the moment in the printed word trapped between the covers of a book. However, John writes very much as he speaks, and he speaks very much as he lives.

Most of what you find in these pages is therefore never cheap, often cheerful, infuriatingly orthodox, and persistently encouraging.

† MICHAEL MARSHALL

Acknowledgments

GRATITUDE is due first and last to the congregation of my beautiful church on Fifth Avenue, New York City. Their expectations of the preacher, their capacity to listen and respond, their sharp observations and supportive questions have elicited from me an eagerness to preach and teach that I never knew I could have. In addition, I want to thank my secretary, Dorothy Reynolds, who for years had the Monday morning task of typing up a hand-written manuscript. Cheryl Steiner undertook the heavy job of retyping the lot so that my friend Sam Eerdmans could be sent an acceptable package.

Backing me up, week by week and year after year, have been my priestly colleagues led by the vicar of St. Thomas, Fr. Gary Fertig, whose management of every sort of parochial detail has left me less distracted than I might have been, and thus less tired when the weekly sermon days came around. I have been the beneficiary of their homiletical skills and insights and for that good fortune I am deeply grateful.

Introduction

I was twenty-eight when I fell in love. It was Friday, May 8, 1959, my fourth day in the United States as a curate in Rumson, New Jersey. My new rector had taken me to see something of New York, and after coffee at Schrafft's we went a few blocks north into "one of the finest churches in America," Saint Thomas, Fifth Avenue.

Most of the English cathedrals were known to me. But I was taken aback by this place, with all its splendor, its familiarity, as if it and I had known each other forever. The mutual recognition hit me with the force of a blow, and I knelt where I was. I got up knowing that its life and my life were in some way to be shared. When I came out, I was secretly betrothed.

To what a partner! This graceful, beautiful place had been conceived after a divinely inspired imprudence. After the church had burned almost to the ground in 1905, its grieving people rallied to rebuild the Victorian brownstone and had raised a large sum by April 1906, when the earthquake devastated San Francisco. Hours later, the parish priest called the St. Thomas vestrymen together and asked what the restoration fund contained. One million, two hundred thousand, he was told. "Gentlemen, we have five dollars in the fund. I telegraphed the rest to San Francisco this morning for the victims of the earthquake. They need it more than we do." The following day the story appeared in the New York papers. The response was swift: money poured in. Within ten days, one million four hundred thousand dollars had been given by people of all faiths and none. Plans to rebuild were put aside. Instead, this extraordinary child of Ralph Adams Cram and Bertram Goodhue was born. Not neo-Gothic. Gothic. Mysteriously, the flame of Gothicism had leaped five centuries and four thousand miles, to burn gloriously on Fifth Avenue. No architectural detail escaped the loving attention of its creators. Money kept coming in, in glad gratitude for the rector's reckless charity. The church stands in its resurrection beauty on the corner of Fifty-third Street, white and shining, the quiet Christ reigning in majesty as he surveys the clamor and frantic push of the crowds along the avenue.

For fifteen years I have been its priest and rector—and its lover. Never a day passes without my admiring something in it or on it. People comment on its extraordinary "feel." Empty, its glory soars. Full, as often it is, it has the look of a cathedral with the friendliness of a country church. It can take all the color and pageantry and precision of the high ceremonial. Its music is unsurpassed in this country; we have the genius of Dr. Gerre Hancock and his wife, Judith, to thank for that. Of course, we are fortunate to have the only church choir school, a boarding school for boy choristers, in this country. Their voices give joy to thousands in the records they produce. The music ought to be good.

Never think that all this powerful beauty reduces the worshipers to quiet passivity. The congregational response is unlike anything I have ever heard in the Anglican world. People who have been to the Easter liturgies will tell you that the shout affirming the Lord's resurrection, and the singing of the hymns, is startling, electrifying. When you have over three thousand people praising God with joyful voice, singing "as one," as the Bible says; as the smell of the incense blends with the scent of the great urns of flowers, the place filled with candle flame, you will know to what heights worship can lift you.

This active response is just as noticeable when the congregation listens to God's Word, read and preached. Week after week, year after year, my joy has been to try to tell my family of worshipers of the secrets and the message of God. Their encouragement, always seasoned with the salt of their acute and intelligent critical faculties, has called from us who minister to them more than we were aware we had to give. For that, I can never be too grateful. They expect a lot from us. They are right to expect that hard work and hours of clear thinking are spent in the preparation of sermons.

You may like to know how I work at mine. After thirty years in the priesthood, I still average a half hour for every minute I preach; hence, eight hours on a sixteen-minute sermon. Mine are written in longhand on the best paper, for I am writing a letter to God, about him and his Son, with the help of the Holy Spirit. The demand never stops and I worry as I always have until it is as ready as it can be (but never finished). Being a morning person helps. I am often busy at five o'clock, pruning it, rewriting it after a night's sleep. I love doing this.

This book is an anthology of fifteen years' preaching effort at St. Thomas. Cowardice, laziness, procrastination, and the general distractions of a parish life that fascinates me have effectively prevented the effort to get it into some sort of shape until now. But two men named Michael have finally pulled me around. The first is Michael Ramsey, that legend of an archbishop of Canterbury. For reasons known only to God and himself, he appointed me in 1960 as his chaplain when he was archbishop at York. The next decade, most of it, I spent as his son and servant, and am the beneficiary of his patient example and direct teaching. If ever asked for my educational background, I would put, "Educated by Michael Ramsey, archbishop of Canterbury, after Oxford." In the middle of a life of appalling distractions as Primate of All England and the first among equals of the Anglican Communion, this man would write books, pellucid as crystal, deep in their simplicity, with a surety of touch his speech often belied. He *knew* what he wrote about. He lived it. I have seen him at his private nastiest and I think he is a bit of a saint. He never stopped thinking. Who of us can really claim that? Ruminating in cars, on journeys, in rooms full of people expecting him to be chatty, at state banquets, in his stall in Lambeth Palace Chapel, often during the working hours (which were endless), I would find him thinking things through. You can read the results. His fecundity shamed me, especially when I was under his roof and could see him producing sermons and speeches and addresses and articles. And books. He is the icon of the Episcopate for us Anglicans: learned, saintly, articulate, silent, unaffected by "every wind and blast of vain doctrine" to blow across the churches and still utterly open to what the Spirit may be saying to them. No one can match him. His loving knowledge of the Scriptures, the way he uses them, expounds them, turns them to face a certain light so that they shine, always crystal clear and phrased in the simplest manner possible, set him aside as a teacher of the rarest quality. He is utterly unafraid, often uncompromising in the challenge his preaching and teaching bring to bear on his disciples. He speaks for God and you know it.

The second Michael is a young English bishop. Years ago, I heard him define certain *desiderata* for a bishop: "Aged, patriarchal, and silent." This young, articulate, and occasionally voluble man found himself a bishop at thirty-seven. Michael Marshall is seven books down with two, at least, on the stocks. They have sold well, some very well, and many beginners in the Christian pilgrimage have him to thank for his effective guidance. As a close friend and colleague in the Anglican Institute, which he directs with such skill and effectiveness, I can testify to his *capacity for vitalization.* It comes from a place and a Person beyond him. We stand in awe of the spiritual energy of this man. He is provocative, sometimes maddeningly so. But he forces us to think. Robust in the happy vigor of his faith, he comforts us, in the real meaning of the term: he imparts strength. God's strength. If he regards me as he says he does as more terrifying than the old archbishop of Canterbury, then I regard him as my catalyst. He released in me the determination to do something about a book. Encouragement is a secret weapon of his. The preaching at St. Thomas he knows. He visits often, and we are one of the Anglican Institute parochial centers. He wants me to tell you what I have been telling my people all these years.

And what is that? Archbishop Michael Ramsey taught me the effectiveness of enlightened traditionalism: the faith of the Catholic Church as Anglicanism has received it, reverence for Scripture and tradition, and a lively social conscience in its application. No conservative, he. Nor am I, particularly.

The people I care for and serve are a remarkable lot. "From every nation under heaven," they have become family members of St. Thomas Church. From every conceivable social and educational background, too. By no means are they prosperous, middle-class and middle-aged. I have discovered what I think is a phenomenon. Coming Sunday by Sunday and committed to Christ and what we stand for in this part of the church are growing numbers of younger men and women, approximately 24-35 years old, who are questioning and looking for answers they once thought they possessed. If I look carefully at the lives they have been living, I notice that frequently they have experienced a setback, a disappointment, a catastrophe, which has caught them in midflight. They have lost the job for which they were confident they were God's gift. A love affair has blown up in their faces. A marriage has failed, mysteriously and grievously. A triumphal pursuit has, one way or another, been checked, blocked, or diverted, and they find they have to settle for something else, somebody else. Almost always there is some point of humiliation or defeat from which they have had to start again. What they had imagined were their strengths are no longer seen as such. What these reversal phenomena demonstrate in fact is the utter failure of what my friend and former parishioner, Professor Paul Vitz, describes in his book *Psychology as Religion—The Cult of Self Worship* (Eerdmans, 1977) as "selfism." The whole business of an inflated, self-taught, self-sustaining ego that can be built up with the aid of helpful little books and, sadly, by some clergymen preaching this technique (and bending or obscuring the stark claims of the gospel of Christ to do it) is held up to criticism that is merciless in its accuracy of aim.

Vitz puts his finger on a need I have noticed in these people who turn to the church for reassurance or reminder of a dimension beyond what they had calculated for the perspectives previously assumed by them, and now found to be faulty, fragile, and foolish. In the tenth chapter, "Beyond the Secular Self," he writes:

> The justification for these concepts has been lost, and reeducation is desperately needed. We need updated orthodox theology. We need sermons on radical obedience, on the mysticism of submissive surrender of the will, on the beauty of dependency, on how to find humility. We all know it is hard for a rich man to get to heaven; I'm certain that it is even harder for a Ph.D. The problem for a Ph.D.—and I really mean to include doctors and lawyers and professionals of all types—is the problem of pride and will.

> Please, I would like to hear something that would improve my odds! (P. 129)

What has made my attempt to answer this need such a joy has been the quality of *listening*. People listen to me closely. Part of the reason for this is that my English accent and vocabulary may be a challenge for American ears. But our parishioners listen hard to everyone who preaches—a fact noticed by visitors in the pews and pulpit alike. This kind of reception to what is being said elicits the best from a preacher, as my colleagues all realize. They inspire me too with what they have to say, and work hard to say it well. I owe them a great debt as I see them respond to the legitimate expectation of the crowd of people sitting below them.

When Jacob had wrestled with the angel of God the night through, he limped from his encounter into the dawn, a theologian. He had learned a thing or two about God. The pain and the indignity were all part of that exercise. There is no easy way, no painless way, of discovering the truths of who God is. Nothing in this enterprise is cheap. If it *is* cheap, we have somehow missed the real point. Those of us who have heard of the uselessness of cheap grace would affirm that there is no way of telling about Christ without his cross and all that led up to it. There is no way of proclaiming divine forgiveness without warning of the burn of shame as repentance begins and the turning around to God takes us back to him. Pain to our pride is part of our experience of God. C. S. Lewis speaks about this all the time. His uncomfortable habit of making me face these issues has had a deep effect upon me. He has, times without number, pinned me mercilessly to face an issue so that I am unable even to blink in order to shut its presence out. What other contemporary writer could put the truth so vividly? I read him again and again. A paragraph, a mere sentence, will start me thinking furiously. He is a needlesome companion; he gives me little rest. Without knowing it, I find myself saying things he has pricked me into thinking.

Similarly, the writings of Austin Farrer, another great Anglican protagonist, never fail to make me think. I knew him as an undergraduate, when I listened to his lectures at Trinity. I heard him preach several times. That frail, forgettable face, bereft of much color, would shine as people strained to hear the torrent of words quietly pouring out. At times devastatingly funny, his musings always from a quarter least expected, delicately phrased with a philosopher's balance; they fed our souls and put our minds through hard exercise. Was ever there a definition of divine forgiveness more poignant and more powerful than his?

> God forgives me, for he takes my head between his hands and turns my face to his to make me smile at him. And though I struggle and hurt those hands—for they are human, though divine, and scarred with nails—though I hurt them, they do not let go until he has smiled me into smiling; and that is the forgiveness of God. (*Said or Sung* [Faith Press, 1960], p. 59)

This definition has devastated me and rebuilt me more often this past quarter of a century than any other. It says it all.

I wish people knew the Bible better. Biblical illiteracy is almost total among Episcopalians. If we loved Scripture we would remember it. As it is, it is no longer educationally fashionable to learn things by heart. *By heart,* from the seat of the affections, from the fount of will and motive. It has been part of my mission and ministry at St. Thomas to impart my love for Scripture and to help my family here to realize that in the Psalms, for instance, we can have the same access to a spiritual treasure box as Christ himself had when he learned them as a boy. People rarely pick up the Bible. But I will never stop hoping, and never stop trying, to make God's Word known and loved and used by his people here. We have Bibles in the pews, to help. We are careful with the way we read it publicly. And all of us try to preach biblically. No time for politics from the pulpit. There is far too much to tackle without resorting to political diatribe. Keep that for the forum, where there is right of reply.

Put all this teaching and preaching in a setting of worship as magnificent as we can make it. Generosity and hospitality are marks of catholicism, and it has been my unswerving will and purpose to make sure that the worship we offer is the very finest, musically, liturgically, as well as homiletically, of which we are capable. You may find in this book what I think about that. It is our top priority, preeminent above everything else we can do—above even works of mercy. We shall be what we shall be because we worship what we worship. We are affected at our very deepest by what we pay homage to. I have banged this drum until my arm is sore. And I am sorry not one bit. People have heard: they know it. They say it. They pay for it—gladly. The response of the congregation is in all kinds of service, often sacrificial, to people beyond our doors who need help of one sort or another. I am proud of them. But then I am a family man. God has given me this lovely family to serve and nurture. Strong-minded, generous, as different as chalk from cheese, many of them; yet all with a family likeness, as they grow "unto the measure of the stature of the fulness of Christ" (Eph. 4:13).

This place, this family, is the joy of my life. I am a happy priest. People know it, and often remark about it. Not that the happiness is free from the anxieties, frustrations, disappointments, and betrayals that are the daily bread of a priest. They are there, many that are secret and borne in a silence shared with Christ whose "visage is marred more than any man's," and who understands more about the hurts of humanity than the rest of the world put together. Ministering to this joy through my life has been a line of faithful Christians who by forgiveness, acceptance, encouragement, chastisement, example, and prayers have required me to think, have taught me, given me hope, reduced me to size, made me more aware of and have held up God's way for me to walk in. Whereof I rejoice. And I want you to share something of this joy in the encouragement I try to bring.

Nothing *Cheap* and Much that is *CHEERFUL*

First Things First

THE ability to spot priorities is a gift many envy. Well they may; it is an aspect of wisdom, and it is essential. I often recall my first rector when I began my ministry. In the late thirties, as Europe lurched into war, he had been what was then described as Senior Air Warden. One night he was alerted by telephone that bombers were approaching the coast, and as he was dressing, the alarm sounded. The noise of approaching aircraft grew louder, and he heard the janitor's wife come down the rectory stairs from their top-floor apartment, calling up to her husband, "Harry, come on down; they're coming over." A muffled voice upstairs: "I can't. I've lost me dentures." The wife: "Get yourself down. They're dropping bombs, not bloody sandwiches."

See how important Christ thinks it is to establish priorities from what St. Matthew tells us in his Gospel: "And now some men brought him a paralysed man lying on a bed. Seeing their faith Jesus said to the man, 'Take heart, my son; your sins are forgiven'" (Matt. 9:2, NEB). Aren't you surprised? Wouldn't you have expected Christ to heal him first and then to absolve him from sin? Jesus does not explain. He looks, and he knows what he must do first to *save* this paralytic.

Examine Christ's scale of priorities. The first is not wholeness. It is holiness. This is disconcerting because in our preoccupation with physical health and mental well-being we think we are right to emphasize the preeminence of wholeness, for life. But Christ's mission is salvation, nothing less. That is the redemption not merely of physical failure and mental malaise but of the whole world of creation, physical and spiritual. This cosmic concept is stupendous, and human wholeness is part of it. But only part. Christ's concern here with holiness before wholeness brings a bewildering realm of priorities to our notice. They are the Divine Priorities.

One of the many things I love about our Lord is his passion for taking pains with us, helping us to see what he is up to. Christ wants to show us. He wants to share this with us. He takes a man; he exposes him first to forgiveness, divine forgiveness. The depths of that experience, as well we know, cannot be plumbed, for in the end the merits that have to be acknowledged in favor of a soul needing God's forgiveness are infinitesimal compared with the standards of God's holiness. We are forced to describe that poetically as "a refiner's fire," which on its approach reduces human pretense and human pride to dust and ashes, leaving the object of his judgment purified as well as reduced. Somehow this fire, this living, loving flame, embraces us, surrounds us, sears us, enlivens us, lights up his flame again in our smoky souls, and gently mends us for our part in his purposes of cosmic salvation.

So he absolves the paralytic; he declares the divine forgiveness over him. What for? We are not told. The helpless can make life hell for those who look after them. Their demands and their self-centeredness, while understandable, can still be terrible. I have never forgotten a nurse who told me of the effects upon her personality that her patients' endless demands have caused. The weak are not harmless. This is a fact of life and we must recognize it. I said once to an old parishioner, who was almost bedridden and very spiritually aware, "Be good!" She asked how she could be otherwise in her condition. I was able to tell her what I have just told you. She saw, *because she knew.*

Holiness before wholeness. It is an unfamiliar priority to a nation that places a premium upon well-being. On Tuesdays at St. Thomas we always have spiritual healing as part of the midday Eucharist. That is deliberate. These services are placed within the setting of the Holy Communion, where we come primarily to be "ransomed, healed, restored, forgiven." What happens there to the soul who comes obedient to his "word, to feast on Heavenly food"? Listen to the verses of that lovely hymn:

Here, O my Lord, I see thee face to face;
Here would I touch and handle things unseen;
Here grasp with firmer hand th' eternal grace,
And all my weariness upon thee lean.

Here would I feast upon the bread of God;
Here drink with thee the royal wine of heav'n;
Here would I lay aside each earthly load;
Here taste afresh the calm of sin forgiv'n.

Is not this precisely the order of priorities such as Christ himself has set? Holiness before wholeness—both integral parts of the salvation he comes to bring, but the second very much a part of the first, and the first indispensable to the second for its effectiveness. When Christ heals he not merely restores life to what it should be; he imparts *his* strength and *his* purity to the sick—and what is that but his holiness? It was a saint of old, Theophilus bishop of Antioch, who declared,

> Hear further, O man, of the work of resurrection going on in yourself. Even though you were unaware of it. For perhaps you have sometimes fallen sick, and lost flesh, and strength, and beauty, but *when you received again from God mercy and healing*—mercy and healing—you picked up again in flesh and appearance and recovered also your strength.

Holiness before wholeness, one of the Divine Priorities. Are there others? Many. Reflect upon the times when Christ himself stated priorities. I can only give you some, but you can be sure that a considerable portion of his teaching was spent in helping people to establish priorities, divine and human. Of the man on his way to church with hatred in his heart for someone: "*First* be reconciled to your brother, and only then come and offer your gift at the altar." To those whose delight it was to see faults and sins in others: "*First* take the plank out of your own eye and then you will see clearly to take the speck out of your brother's eye." When talking of the havoc wrought by the forces of evil among good and promising souls whom he likens to good seed sown in the ground and "tares" being sown among it by an enemy, he says, "Let them both grow together till harvest, and at harvest time I will tell the reapers 'Gather the "tares" *first,* and tie them in bundles for burning, then collect the wheat into my barn.'" And again, "This is the *first* and great commandment. . . ." To the rich young man who wanted to be with him: "*First* sell what you have, and give to the poor." To those who found the woman in the act of her adultery: "Let him who is without sin cast the *first* stone." To self-righteous Pharisees: "*First* clean the inside of the cup, then the outside will be clean also." In fact he reserves his most searing term for those whose spiritual priorities are misplaced, when he calls the Scribes and Pharisees "whited sepulchres."

Christ wants us to face up to the realm of spiritual realities that we must acknowledge if we really want to know him better. He never talks of "finding yourself" (in the way we are forever doing, especially when referring to students who drop out of school in order to do just that) without telling us that we must first lose ourselves, for only he who loses his life shall find it—his. Through his teaching, through his life, the great tenor bell of the Divine Priorities sounds: "Seek ye *first* the kingdom of God." It is this challenge, this requirement, that has to be met if we mean business. And the priorities he expresses are geared for just this.

There was one young man for whom these priorities came to mean everything. He too was a rich young man, and the Lord's words found the door of his heart: "*First* sell all you have and give to the poor." For him that meant his heritage, his family, as well as his possessions. He had plenty. And he had a love of life that he never lost and the girls found him fascinating. His high spirits brought him into street fights as well as into quick romances. He went off and joined the army and for a year was a prisoner of war. His last name was Bernardone and his first became one of the best loved in the world—Francis, to be known as Saint Francis only two years after his death: October 4 is his Feast Day. It was gospel priorities that hit him one day and he was never the same again. Around Umbria he traveled, fired by the priorities that convicted him, seeking first God's kingdom. He changed the whole aspect of things as he touched the hearts of men and women. He began to exhibit the power to distinguish Divine Priorities, and others learned them from him because he first lived them through. Only so could he pray:

> *O Divine Master,*
> *grant that I may not seek so much*
> *to be consoled as to console;*
> *to be understood as to understand;*
> *to be loved as to love.*
> *For it is in giving that we receive;*
> *it is in pardoning that we are pardoned;*
> *and it is in dying that we are born to eternal life.*

Love, the Setting for Lent

I remember once when there was particular excitement at the Metropolitan in New York—and with good reason. An opera with a plot of dubious historical accuracy but marvelously singable music was to be staged for the first time in many years, and Sutherland and Pavarotti were in it. The house was full, expectant, as *I Puritani* began; the setting was magnificent, and what followed that evening justified the hopes of all present—down to the last opera buff.

The setting, I said, was magnificent: a Puritan castle near Plymouth. One glance was enough to prepare us. It set the mood, it brought us in, it started the imagination flying, it did not distract us, it made us listen. It did in fact what a setting should do.

Each year Ash Wednesday brings the season of fasting and abstinence to us, a time for the examination of the heart, when we pray that there may be created and made in us new and contrite hearts; God knows we need them.

The business of creating in us a new and a contrite heart is costly. There is no such thing as cheap creation. A new heart, a contrite heart. The heart of which the Prayer Book Collect speaks, the heart the Scriptures so often describe, is not so much that tiny organ, that insignificant-looking thing which pumps blood through the body, as the wellspring within us which floods our attitudes, our aspirations, our desires, our morals, our achievements. That heart floods all these and provides the stream which carries us to our destiny. For it is from the heart that love comes; we love *from the heart,* and whom we love and how we love and when and where we love make us who we are and what we are and whose we are as possessors and possessed. There lies our destiny. There in the heart. Our life's purpose and its fulfillment or final emptiness, our true identity which no disguise of personality can hide, are all bound up in this and there is no escape from the direction our heart sets us upon. A new heart, then, and a contrite heart is what the Scriptures tell us we need, and what the church knows us to need; knows, and provides the opportunity for us to be given. Lent is a season of crisis.

It is a season of crisis because the desire or the repugnance for a new heart goes to the deepest depths of the human soul for the source and wellspring to be cleaned and purified. Did not our Lord say some stern things exactly about this to the Scribes and Pharisees who were harassing him: "Wicked thoughts, murder, adultery, fornication, theft, perjury, slander—these all proceed from the heart; and these are the things that defile a man" (Matt. 15:19-20, NEB). Lent is a time to tackle that condition, and we come on Ash Wednesday to start. First we look back, back far beyond the time our Lord walked in Galilee, back to the very earliest accounts of man coming to terms with himself and God and we offer to administer the symbol of humankind's humiliation and penitence, the Ashes. Of all the human symbols the Ashes are among the most ancient and in their simplicity the most eloquent; for as they denote the worthlessness of what remains when fire has consumed a substance, so they denote the worth of human ambition and achievement when it is besmirched with pride and disobedience to the loving demands of a loving God. They are the result of the pure fire of the divine judgment having come upon that pride-soiled ambition and achievement. That is the place to start this season of crisis: with being *made to see* a symbol of the divine judgment upon the ambitions and achievements of a heart "as fat as brawn," a heart "hardened," a "stony" heart, a "froward" heart (all of which are scriptural terms). The smudge is visible, at least for a time, and the time is long enough to remember two things: the fact that a fellow sinner like yourself has been prepared to say "sorry" to God for having misused his love—that is what sin is all about—and the fact that having apologized, the soul repents, turns again, determines to amend for past failures and wrongdoing, and seeks God's help and grace—a costly grace.

The smudge of ashes on the brow,
The charge, "Remember, man, that thou
Art dust, and shalt to dust return—"
These are the words, the dictum stern
Of Elohim, relayed in rite
The ages down, to hearts contrite.
Remember then, O Ichabod,
That dust thou art, gold dust for God.

Francis Lightbourn

I love that. It encourages me through the judgment. "*Gold dust for God*" who loves us as he judges us, who loves us as he requires from us nevertheless certain responses to his love, and our judgment centers on what we do with that love of his, poured into our hearts. We spurn his love when we substitute our own standards for those his love sets. We squander his love when we love ourselves more than we love the people he has placed around us and in our lives. We cheapen his love when we love others cheaply. We pervert his love when our love becomes possessive. We make the fire of his love smoky with our lusts, we tarnish his love when we love things for their own sake. We reflect his love in our moments of patient love, in our sacrificial, self-effacing love, in our love of noble causes and in our enduring love of those who suffer.

The fire of the divine judgment, which is God's love burning its righteous path through history, comes near to us. As it does, our hearts respond to the warmth of that fire of love. Our judgment lies in those responses, and in being required by that righteous love to face their consequences, stern and even horrifying as those consequences might be.

I have for years been pondering the mystery of the divine judgment upon us. The more I think about it and read what the Bible has to tell me and consider the lives of people who have taken their faith seriously, the more certain I am that set deep within this mystery—and probably at its very heart—are the effects of how we return that majesty of outpoured love—the quality of it, the quantity of it, or its total absence. All these effects go to make us what we are and what we shall become. "A broken and a contrite heart, O God, shalt thou not despise" is the prayer of the soul alive and aware of the divine judgment as on Ash Wednesday and through Lent it pays attention to what it does with God's love. And that is what Lent is all about. It is not a temporary abstinence from a habit, like smoking; not a temporary switching to tomato juice without the vodka; not a Dover sole for lunch in place of a veal cutlet; not a forty-day regret to cocktail party invitations along with advance notice of a plan for a smash on Easter Day. Fasting and abstinence do not mean the substitution of one delicious item for another any more than they imply a temporary moratorium from cherished possessions like a family feud or an illicit love affair. Lent means the observance of means which are not ends in themselves, means which are costly in order to be given a new heart and to put things right because of it. The early Hebrews rarely minced words; they used few euphemisms and their language was graphic. To our ears, to our careful hygienic American hearing, such language can shock. I don't shock for the sake of shock, but I want to quote a phrase from Scripture which is devastating: "Circumcise the foreskin of your heart . . ." (Deut. 10:16). This is a surgical act, an act of separation by a sharp knife, a cutting away, the shedding of blood, and the cause of some pain. Furthermore, it signifies submission to a law divinely given, a law given nevertheless by the God of love, to make plain and beyond all doubt that a requirement has been complied with. The rest of the sentence reads "and be no longer stubborn." There's Lent for you. But the setting for it? You will recall what I said about the setting to *I Puritani:* one glance was enough to prepare us. It set the mood, it brought us in, it started the imagination flying, it did not distract us; it made us listen.

So read again that hauntingly beautiful thirteenth chapter of Paul's first letter to the Corinthians. It is all about love; God's love dwelling in us, our hearts the wellspring within us which floods our attitudes, our aspirations, our desires, our morals, our achievements, providing the stream that carries us to our destiny. For our destiny to be in him we have to have *his* love, purified and life-giving, in us. And then perhaps again that familiar prayer, "O Lord who hast taught us that all our doings without charity [love] are nothing worth, send thy Holy Ghost, and pour into our hearts that most excellent gift of love, the very bond of peace and all virtues, without which whosoever liveth is counted dead before thee."

For the setting for Lent is love, God's for us of course before ours for him. The church has purposely done this. That setting is essential, in the real meaning of that term—it is the substance of its real being. For to live, the contrite heart, the new heart, has to be fed from that source. Here is a prayer for you:

Repentance

LORD, when for joy I seek thy Presence,
give me a godly sorrow for my sins;
yea, and for my righteousnesses also.

O Lord that my sins may be covered,
strengthen me to uncover them
honestly, unsparingly,
before thine infinite love.

Let my heart with all its secrets
be thrown as open to thee
as thy mercies to me.

May I never confess my faults
with no purpose to leave them
nor make half-repentances,
lest I make none.

Rather let me lift up to thee
all my prides and shames,
the stubborn and the small,
the recurrent and the continuous,
that they may be buried low,
and have no resurrection.

Eric Milner-White
*(*My God, My Glory *[SPCK, 1967] p. 24)*

To Keep a True Lent

I wonder if you know the poem, "To Keep a True Lent"? The poem is curious. It is modern. It is up to the minute. It is over three hundred years old. Its secret? Its author loved life with a passion. He loved love, too, spiritual and physical. I should have loved to know him, for he was very real, very honest, and he enjoyed people and beauty. You really need to read it aloud—and listen as you read it.

Is this a Fast, to keep
The Larder leane?
And cleane
From the fat of Veales and Sheep?

Is it to quit the dish
Of Flesh, yet still
To fill
The platter high with Fish?

Is it to faste an houre,
Or rag'd to go,
Or show
A downcast look, and sowre.

No: 'tis a Fast, to dole
Thy sheaf of wheat
And meat
Unto the hungry soule.

It is to fast from strife,
From old debate,
And hate;
To circumcise thy life.

To shew a heart grief-rent;
To starve thy sin,
Not Bin;
And that's to keep thy Lent.

Robert Herrick knew what he was talking about; he wrote as a *lover of life*. Furthermore, and let us not be unduly and falsely modest about this, he was an Anglican. Perhaps we do not assert this sufficiently, but at a time when the church is in danger of losing her nerve and her temper over vexatious issues and reverses and embarrassing disobediences, she could well remind herself that there is much in her history and in contemporary events to commend the Anglican way of looking at things and doing things. For at their best, *at their best*, those ways, those Anglican approaches, are wise, they are adult, they are serious, and they can be stern without being miserable, requiring the faithful believers to use their heads, steering between the Puritan's distrust of life's joys:

The Puritan through life's sweet garden goes
To pluck the thorn and cast away the rose,
And hopes to please by this peculiar whim
The God who fashioned it and gave it him.

Kenneth Hare

Steering between that—and between a patronizing unwillingness to give anything but pat answers and rigid formulae to thoughtful souls who want something more: Long live the Anglican approach, I say, to the things of the spirit and of the body.

And Lent concerns both spirit and body. Each year the church provides an opportunity for spirit and body to embrace in a period of fasting and abstinence. Soul and body need it, both. And both need to welcome it, not merely to endure it. They need to welcome it not for masochistic reasons in order to be miserable, but because it is a wonderful opportunity for God to work powerfully in hearts that are receptive and open to his working. In St. Paul's phrase we may hope to "grow into the measure of the stature of the fullness of Christ." Christ wants us to grow into his fullness—into the fullness of his abundant life. He wants us for himself, to realize our potential as fully and properly human—as a preparation for our companionship in eternity with him—properly human, which we are not. At least not yet. Not with the fatty degeneration of our soul from which none of us is free. Our pride, our self-pity, our predilections, our preferences, our rages, and our resentments prevent that growth, and until we love him more and ourselves less we shall never grow. Lent is the time to tackle the fatty degeneration of the soul. So see again how Herrick views Lent:

Is this a Fast, to keep
The Larder leane?
And cleane
From the fat of Veales and Sheep?

Is it to quit the dish
Of Flesh, yet still
To fill
The platter high with Fish?

Is it to faste an houre,
Or rag'd to go,
Or show
A downcast look, and sowre.

Humorously and maturely he puts his finger on silly pharisaism, the pharisaism Christ exposed as unworthy and fundamentally dishonest because it is trivial; straining at gnats and swallowing camels.

> Be careful not to make a show of your religion before men; if you do, no reward awaits you in your Father's house in heaven.
>
> Thus, when you do some act of charity, do not announce it with a flourish of trumpets, as the hypocrites do in synagogue and in the streets to win admiration from men. I tell you this: they have their reward already. No; when you do some act of charity, do not let your left hand know what your right is doing; your good deed must be secret, and your Father who sees what is done in secret will reward you.
>
> Again, when you pray, do not be like the hypocrites; they love to say their prayers standing up in synagogue and at the street corners, for everyone to see them. I tell you this: they have their

> reward already. But when you pray, go into a room by yourself, shut the door, and pray to your Father who is there in the secret place; and your Father who sees what is secret will reward you. . . .
>
> So too when you fast, do not look gloomy like the hypocrites: they make their faces unsightly so that other people may see that they are fasting. I tell you this: they have their reward already. But when you fast, anoint your head and wash your face, so that men may not see that you are fasting, but only your Father who is in the secret place; and your Father who sees what is secret will give you your reward. (Matt. 6:1-6, 16-18, NEB)

Why go without meat in order to plan a lobster dinner? Why go without your cocktail in order to plan a party to end all parties on Easter evening? Why refrain from smoking if abstinence from it makes you bad tempered, liable to kick the cat, and impossible to live with for six weeks, moaning and whining and full of self-pity the whole time? Why spoil penitence with depression instead of hope? Why assume that penitence is alien to joy? Why economize if you keep the rewards of economy for yourself instead of giving it away? And that brings us to verse 4.

No: 'tis a Fast, to dole
Thy sheaf of wheat
And meat
Unto a hungry soule.

Christ recalls us again and again to the need to be sensitive to the sufferings of others. It is not just a matter of fasting from food so that we can help support famine relief—I hope we all do this. Our Lenten self-denial envelopes, our gifts (perhaps sacrificial), should go to the poor and underprivileged and starving thousands. Our lunch money once or twice a week can soon amount to something considerable for others less fortunate. So, not merely hunger for food, but hunger for love. Is there someone who wants our love, in whose face we shut the door of our hearts? Is there someone who is being starved from our affections, when with an effort of will on our side we can open our hearts to that soul? Is there someone who is hurting us and whom we resent for it? Now is the time to consider. Now is the time to open the well-stocked larder of the heart for a restoration, a reconciliation of a broken relationship, a hungry heart. And so to verse 5.

It is to fast from strife,
From old debate,
And hate;
To circumcise thy life.

Is this not profoundly true? Can you not hear the voice of God in all this?

On Ash Wednesday, the day of public penitence and sorrow for having offended God, there is a ceremony of poignant and profound significance, the blessing and distribution of the Ashes upon the forehead. The ceremony has well over a thousand years' history, and ashes as a symbol of sorrow and humiliation go back much further than that, to Old Testament times.

But why ashes? Well, consider what *fire* meant to the people of the Old Testament. It meant the presence of God. Moses was confronted by the bush alight and aflame in the desert of his exodus. The creation story with which Genesis begins tells of the cherubim guarding the way to the tree of life with the flaming sword, God's presence. Against that fire nothing could stand. "Who shall stand when he appeareth?" That fire, the early Jews said, the fire of the presence of God, was unapproachable and even purified further that which was already pure. What is less than pure is reduced to dust after the living fire has gone over it. And what has God to say of the dust that remained? Go back to that terrifying story of the fall of man, the account of human bumptiousness, arrogance, and self-reliance, when God confronts man, and in poetry that can send shivers down the spine, he says:

Accursed be the soil because of you.
With suffering shall you get your food from it
every day of your life.
It shall yield you brambles and thistles,
And you shall eat wild plants.
With sweat on your brow
you shall eat your bread
until you return to the soil,
as you were taken from it.

For dust you are,
And unto dust shall you return.

Dust is God's stern phrase for the worthlessness of the pride of man pitted against himself, when the consuming fire has passed over it. "Dust and Ashes" are the same thing, the worthless remains. So they denote deep humiliation, and the Scriptures have many a reference to them. Job in his misery, struck down from the sole of his foot to the top of his head with malignant boils, took a piece of pot to scrape himself and sat in the ashpit. Mordecai tore his garments in the ancient ritual sign of mourning at blasphemy and put on sackcloth and ashes in his humiliation at unfair legislation proposed in his country.

And so this special sign and symbol have a very real and mysterious significance. On Ash Wednesday when Christians come to the House of God to observe, as a family of God's forgiven sinners, their grief at having offended him, they are confronted with the story of the Fall, for it is precisely these very words which are said: "Remember O man that dust thou art and unto dust shalt thou return." Symbolism is very necessary for us as humans.

So we say we are sorry; and we mean it. God picks us up, in the wonderful way he has with his ready forgiveness, brushes us off, and sends us out to do his will with the reminder as kind as it is stern to pay attention to the way we do it: not to attempt too little, for that is self-indulgence, and not to expect too much, for that is presumption. God loveth a cheerful giver, and he wants us to give ourselves to him and each other in the joyful liberty that comes from our closeness to him.

To shew a heart grief-rent;
To starve thy sin,
Not Bin;
And that's to keep thy Lent.

Some Uncomfortable Words

WHY did you have your private number changed?" asked Mrs. Morris, the wife of my good predecessor, the former rector of St. Thomas, on Friday night after dinner. Why, indeed? "Because a madwoman was calling me at 1:15 in the morning and at 5:45 later the same morning," I said. "If she couldn't sleep, she evidently had determined I shouldn't. So I changed it. If people want me, they can get me at the church's number." Much better arrangement, we all agreed, and then went off into a discussion of a theory Dorothy Morris had about people in Manhattan and indeed the world over wanting for the most part a quiet life when the day's work was over and not really being grateful for telephone calls invading the privacy of their home. We do not cherish invasion. Even the most party-loving, the most gregarious, the most frenetic of us fondly imagine the delights of the quiet life, free from intrusion, abrasion, and the hellish annoyances which jar the pleasurable progress planned by ourselves for our convenience. The life of self-choosing is precious to us. We are answerable to so many: to our colleagues and superiors at work, to the IRS, to the meter maids, to the people who serve us, and to the people who teach us. If we are rich, we are targets for hopeful fund-raisers. If we are poor, we have the rent collector to worry about. It is tempting to dream of a life of quiet from the scratch and irritation of intrusions of people and issues and questions and crises.

In so doing we dream of a world tailored to fit perfectly to ourselves. I once heard a crass love song about "our own little world" proposing this. If the girl being sung to was as boring as the man singing it, it would be some miserable cocoon of an existence and both would be mightily relieved to escape the boredom of the other, the sooner the better.

Into this superficial and selfish daydream of the pleasures of peace, there is a discordant and disturbing voice making itself heard. It is Christ's voice—and what he declares is provocative and surprising and uncharacteristic, especially if you picture him limp and pale pink with a soup plate behind his head and a few dispirited sheep of indeterminate sex at his feet, looking at each other, as stained glass windows so often portray him. He says in uncomfortable words, "You must not think that I have come to bring peace to the earth; I have not come to bring peace, but a sword" (Matt. 10:34).

A sword is for sundering, for dividing in one blow, for dividing into two. It is usually two-edged. Its function is *deadly,* but it can be useful; it can cut deep to get at the truth. King Solomon, you may remember, called for one when two harlots claimed the same child after one baby had died. Each claimed it as her own and accused the other woman of lying. He called for his sword and raised it, as he said, to cut the child into halves, one half for each. One woman declared his intention to be plain justice; the other, the real mother, said, "If this is justice, let *her* have the child, only save its life." She was the real mother and the sword was used to cut to the truth. The true mother was given her true child.

"I have come to bring a sword." He used that sword for getting at the truth, for getting us to face that truth, to live that truth, because living it is living *him.* The peace he is out to disturb is the twilight peace of the coward, the lazy, the expedient, the compromising soul who wants his religion on his terms, who wants his God his size, who wants his fellowmen a smaller size so that they can be managed, manipulated, got around, and finally got rid of quietly. But Christ is here among us with his sword to separate us from our worse selves *because he wants us with our better selves* and knows we work better for him when we travel light. If he will smite the sinews of our propensity for compromise and expediency he will use the other edge on the bones of our continual desire to make bargains with him as a condition for serving him. It is no good telling him, "Love me, love my dog," when my dog is my cherished sin. He brings the blade down upon our satisfaction with the "natural," the earthy, the unsatisfactory in our lives. He refuses to accept that satisfaction. He is looking for sparks within us of divine *dis*satisfaction with ourselves, divine *dis*content with what we have done and where we think we are going. He is looking for the marks of the supernatural in us, the marks of conflict with self, with our life's birthmark, pride, with self-assertion, self-pity, self-aggrandizement, self-satisfaction, self-sufficiency, and self-excusing. He wants to cut us free from ourselves and from self. It is a struggle he himself has been through, when he "learned obedience in the school of suffering" which ended with his willingness to allow his own will to be overruled by that of the Father's will, to give himself to the death of the cross as the last act of self-shorn obedience. He is the peerless example of self shorn from self.

He holds the sword. He *is* the sword. He is in himself the divider of ourselves as well as the unifier, the sunderer of our easy peace as well as the source of our true peace. Do you remember the verse from the letter to the Hebrews: "For the word of God is alive and active. It cuts more keenly than any two-edged sword, piercing as far as the place where life and spirit, joints and marrow, divide. It sifts the purposes and thoughts of the heart" (Heb. 4:12)? The word of God has a lowercase "w." Make it a capital "W" and there is another name for Christ: the Word. He is alive and active. He cuts more keenly than any two-edged sword (made by human hands), piercing as far as the place where life and spirit, joints and marrow, divide.

As we look at him described so truly and mysteriously in those phrases, we hear an ancient echo from the prophet: "Choose ye this day whom ye shall serve," for he embodies the *now,* the present, the urgency of decision, as challenger and challenged, as he brandishes this sword.

Discipleship, for this is what this uncomfortable word is all about, is not merely costly. It is painful and difficult because there is sword-work involved and we are required to submit to it. To do so we have to permit Christ to come very close to us, to work within us. Nearer than arm's length, nearer than sword's reach, in us. He has come, and he brings it among us and brandishes it before us, to divide us from ourselves, our natural selves, our fallen selves, where we take refuge in a peace which is no peace because it is not based on love of the truth. He makes us face issues and face up to ourselves. He cuts with his sword, and smites deep into the bones and sinews of our souls, the areas of our compromise with what is truth about how we live our lives. Do we allow our unfair and cruel prejudices room to grow, and smile upon them as they do so? He cuts into that. Do we foster and hug our pretensions, encouraging others to be awed by them? He cuts into that. Do we quietly stoke the fires of resentment and malice and sit and warm ourselves as those fires glow? He cuts into that. Do we for whatever reason allow someone near us to destroy himself or others because we are frightened of confrontation and want peace at any price? He cuts into that. Do we rationalize our lack of generosity, our failures to forgive? He cuts into that. Do we enjoy the failures of others, telling ourselves that it is good for them to experience humiliation? He cuts into that. Do we get vicarious sexual pleasure from discussing the immoralities of the well known, the highly placed, the enviable? He cuts into that. These are some compromises with the truth which our daily lives may indulge in, and into all these the sword-work must go, to be divided from the heart whose sovereignty he wants to claim

And here, let me tell you a mystery. That dividing, that sundering, that sword-work effects true healing. He smites in order to save us. He brings us together properly when he rends us apart, when he breaks us. It is Divine surgery, which makes for our fullness, our strength, our purity, for it is done with skill, with thoroughness, and above all with true love. Only the soul which has submitted to this can say:

> *For lo, thou requirest truth in the inward parts: . . .*
> *Thou shalt make me hear of joy and gladness*
> *That the bones which thou hast broken may rejoice.*
>
> *Ps. 51:6, 8*

Just Dying to Live!

> The King's first doctor was M. de L'Orme (1584–1678), who had attended Louis XIII and was the fashionable doctor for fifty years. De L'Orme swore by hygiene and applied his theories to himself, with the result that he lived to be ninety-four. "Why do fish live to such great age? Because," said he, "they are never subject to draughts." So he spent his days in a sedan chair draped with blankets and lined with hares' fur to ensure that no air could percolate. When obliged to go out, he covered himself with a morocco robe and mask and wore six pairs of stockings and several fur hats. He always kept a bit of garlic in his mouth, incense in his ears and a stalk of rue sticking out of each nostril. He slept in a sort of brick oven, surrounded by hot water bottles, and lived on sheep's tongues and syrup of greengages—he never touched vegetables, raw fruit, jam or pastry. At eighty-seven he married a young wife; she died within the year.

So wrote Nancy Mitford in that utterly delightful and clever book of hers on Louis XIV of France, *The Sun King*.

Finding out why people do the things they do is an intriguing exercise. The very existence of institutes of behavioral science attests to that. Not only scientists and psychologists—novelists and cartoonists prove it.

I often wonder about St. Paul; why he said what he said and wrote what he wrote. In the second letter he wrote to the church in Corinth, he strings together seven paradoxes, seven seeming contradictions, placing one against another in a description of us all, etching out what it means to commend the cause of Christ in a world either suspicious of him, scornful of him, ignorant of him, unconcerned for him, scandalized by him, or repelled by him. He says this:

> *We are the imposters who speak the truth;*
> *the unknown men whom all men know;*
> *dying we still live on;*
> *disciplined by suffering, we are not done to death;*
> *in our sorrows we have always cause for joy;*
> *poor ourselves, we bring wealth to many;*
> *penniless, we own the world.*
>
> *2 Cor. 6:8-10*

An extraordinary collection. Now, "dying we still live on."

He is talking about something familiar, something he thinks about every day, in his prayers, in his eucharists, in his travels, in his work: *the resurrection experience*. Were it not for that he would not be writing at all, would not be preaching at all, would not be risking his neck, being a fool for Christ. Listen to him: "I am well content, for Christ's sake, with weakness, contempt, persecution, hardship, and frustration; for when I am weak, then I am strong" (2 Cor. 12:10). This is something he not only constantly *thinks* about; this is something he *knows* about. He knows Christ. He has met Christ. In that terrifying, blinding encounter on the Damascus road he has been confronted with the risen Christ, listened to the risen Christ, capitulated to the risen Christ, and as a new slave to the risen Christ has turned about-face, from the pursuit of Christ's people to pursuit of his own: to preach, convince, and win them to his new Master, not by threat of slaughter but by a love which is new to him and a power which though foreign to him yet is natural to him. For his own old self is dead and behold, he lives—lives in the power of Christ's resurrection life. A new man. A changed man, in a world he realizes has been changed by what has happened, for the resurrection world is a world made new. So people have to be told, they have to be shown, have to be prepared—have to die, in some mysterious way, for the resurrection in them to happen. The great cry, "Nevertheless I live—yet not I, for Christ liveth within me" is Paul's discovery cry; the cry of a Christian Archimedes, "Eureka! Eureka! I have found it! I have found it!" It is the experience men have longed for and sighed after—the truth of the promise of Christ. "I am come that they might have life, and that they might have it more abundantly" (John 10:10, KJV). That life, that endless life, is the resurrection life which rests for its truth upon true death; death, not moribundity; death, not suspended animation. "Except a corn of wheat fall into the ground *and die,* it abideth alone: but if it die, it bringeth forth much fruit" (John 12:24, KJV), Christ says; and he knows it is true. There is a stage, a place for death to happen; physically, spiritually, cosmically, it has to happen for the resurrection to happen. For it to happen God has to act—to act as he did with his Son when he raised him from the dead. God's prerogative. God's initiative. Christ first taught it before he experienced it. He knew it was true before he went through it and in joy proved it: "Who for the joy that was set before him endured the cross, despising the shame, and is set down at the right hand of the throne of God" (Heb. 12:2, KJV).

Death began early with Christ—that death to himself and to his own self-pleasing. He started to die to self on the day he was born, when he came into a world which knew him not, came to his own who received him not. Totally without self-assertion, in reticence, in anonymity, in silence he came, content to come in this way. St. Paul, who, as I said, lived thinking and teaching and preaching this concept of Christ's work, describes it in a phrase of sheer genius: Christ came into the world as a man, *emptying himself.* The act of self-emptying could have as its finale one thing and one thing only: death. Jesus chose this, accepted this. He knew without this that no new life could be prepared for, taught and shown, and later rejoiced in. Life, real life, resurrection life, depended on the obedient experience of the acceptance of death. "Bearing the human likeness, revealed in human shape, he humbled himself (emptied himself), and in obedience accepted even death—death on a cross. Therefore God raised him, to the heights (Phil. 2:8), and bestowed on him the name above all names, that at the name of Jesus every knee should bow—in heaven, on earth (that is, the whole creation—it is a cosmic victory) and in the depths—and every tongue confess, 'Jesus Christ is Lord' to the glory of God the Father."

Death came early with his self-emptying, with his self-humiliation. His hidden early life is dead to us. No one knows what he did before his time alone in the wilderness as the new Israel, facing deaths to his pride in the temptations to doubt his integrity, to question the validity of all his certainties and convictions, to be cold, dead to joys he had experienced in the prayer-life and strong spiritual life shared and hidden with God the Father. Speculation is dangerous, and a Christian preacher must beware when he does so in the pulpit. Yet I have wondered many times if one aspect of the indignity and humiliation he went through in his desert temptations had not *of necessity* been some form of death experience of the prayer-life he enjoyed? For his spiritual life temporarily to wither and decay for some time? Could there be a worse death in his life than that? When he would have to search sorrowing for the very thing which made him say and do the things he said and did—that living flame of love that *was* the holy fire of the presence of God? I wonder. I tremble to think of it. But there *was* resurrection. *There was* new life given by God in the soul of Christ, the new Israel in the desert, who could fling back at the tempter the words taken from the Holy Writ of old, words of refutation, words of living and conquering conviction, triumphant words, alive with awareness of where real victory and resurrection-life is to be found. This enlivening awareness, this triumphant insistence in teaching what must happen before new and unending life can be given, springs from the deepest depths of the well of Christ's experience. He knows. He says what he knows. And when he says things like this—things the great St. John seized and treasured and later quoted, the music of heaven can be heard as an accompaniment to it: "The Father loves me because I lay down my life, to receive it back again. No one has robbed me of it; I am laying it down of my own free will. I have the right to lay it down, and I have the right to receive it back again; this charge I have received from my Father" (John 10:17-18).

He knows. He tells us because he wants to help us, who in later centuries have learned from Paul and John and all who have found him, loved him, served him, worshiped him, died for him from loyalty, died in the peace of their experience of a lifetime of allegiance to him. He wants to help us thirst to live this resurrection life, not merely after our departing, our physical death, but in our lives *here and now.* Hence: "As God's servants we try to recommend ourselves . . . dying we still live on." "Dying—and behold, we live." So too, us.

On the stroke of midnight on Wednesday, February 26, 1986, Douglas Webster, a priest, a former canon of St. Paul's Cathedral in London, a friend to many in my parish where for over twelve years he preached and taught and enriched the imaginations of countless people, died after terrible suffering. He died, literally a martyr to cancer which brought him his cross and nailed him on it, and extracted the last ounce of courage and acceptance from him. That such a loving and energetic servant of the Gospel of Christ had this particular cross to bear and later to hang upon is a mystery too deep to plumb for me and all of us who revered him so. But he bravely recognized his cross, and faced it, hung there helpless upon it, and stopped breathing when God's moment for him came.

The legacy he left is not merely in the sermons we kept and published. It is in lives. I know of one person in my congregation who now holds a position of responsibility as a leading layman, whose religious imagination flourishes, and whose perceptions about God and his Son's place in our lives has deeply changed as a result of this man's influence. Certainly I can speak for myself in this regard. What Douglas had to say and tell came from a radical—a root—experience of God which I could discern in him. He had met the Lord along the path and Christ had made himself known powerfully and personally to Douglas, who then made a deep commitment to spread the Good News. Dying, Douglas lives on in the lives he encountered with the message he knew he had to carry. I suppose that this is the stuff that saints are made of: their own faults are alarmingly obvious, and those of us close to Douglas learned, if they did not know already, what a struggle these people have with what we call the old Adam, their lesser selves, warring with their better selves and their better selves winning. It is a fact that all this goes on curiously close to the surface, more transparently fought out than in some of us where our murky depths are perhaps better concealed. His friends were often uncomfortably aware of that intense struggle, but even more aware of the fact that he would die to himself for Christ to live in him; and we are the beneficiaries.

And there are other "deaths." There are times when we have to let a dream die. It may be a political ideal. It may be a greatly cherished hope, such as the hope that your daughter may marry after falling in love with someone you have privately chosen—and in your heart of hearts you think you know what is best for her; and she does not. She falls in love with somebody else, and she goes to live with him, perhaps to marry, perhaps not. Your dream dies. Perhaps it has to die for you to discover something new and wiser about yourself as well as her—and your life is enriched for *that* death.

Or it may be the irrational hope that the disease your loved one has may be miraculously cured, and no cure takes place save the death of your loved one and the death of your irrational hope. Both those deaths are devastating experiences, with bereavement heaped upon despair, though it is not uncommon in human experience that a new dimension of understanding for God's secret ways and sympathy for others can come. That is a form of a new life, of the resurrection of a lively faith.

It may be that in some terrible way you share the experience of many a Christian and find that your beliefs can cost you far more than ever you had imagined. Martyrdom has many forms and faces, but the concerted testimony of the faithful is that new, stronger life leaps from it. In your case it may be the death of a cherished relationship, or even death to a family tie because of your beliefs. A person I heard of left her Jewish faith to become a Christian, and her family actually recited prayers used at the time of death. Her family membership *died.* I well remember how Marie Avinoff, in her autobiography, *Pilgrimage through Hell,* tells of another kind of martyrdom. She suffered it in Soviet Russia when her noble parents, her kinsfolk, her possessions, her reputation, her freedom, her hopes, and finally her own husband were all destroyed in the reign of terror through the years after the 1917 revolution until the Second World War. But in the death of everything and everyone dear to her she discovered in her heart *a resurrection flame,* which consumed her self-pity, her desires for revenge, her bitterness of loneliness and loss. Still she testifies to the power and the wisdom of God.

It is certainly true that there are times when our prayers die, when our love for God and his reality die in "the dark night of the soul." It is a solemn truth that some of us have to experience a death in some part of our spiritual life in order to be given a resurrection life of the Spirit. In this way we are permitted a tiny share in what may well have been our Lord's own experience.

There are things which for Christ's sake we have to *allow* to die—like a relationship which, though not harmful exactly, is not helpful. We all realize this and occasionally we have to "screw our courage to the sticking place" and let the relationship die without hurting or hindering the other soul's progress. The rich young ruler left our Lord's life—he let the young man go. This death can be painful. I've experienced it, and to this day it can hurt. But I know that from the death came a life for each person rightly and deeply freer.

This death is a dying to self, in whatever form it takes, whether it happens to you, whether in conscience you permit it to happen for love of him who gave himself to die. It is a martyrdom of the self, and we not only are vulnerable to it, we *need* it. We need literally to reach that point in life when we just die to live, since there is no other way left to live life.

Lord, when thou wilt and as thou wilt, so that we may share Paul's discovery cry, "Nevertheless I live—yet not I, but Christ liveth within me."

Things Aren't Always What They Seem

YOU have only to go to *La Cage aux Folles* to realize later, if not sooner, that things are not always what they seem. A superficial glance will tell you one thing. A second look may cause you to look yet again, for appearance and reality are not the same. So there is the chance of surprise, sometimes pleasant, sometimes not. The back of a crocodile may look like a log in a river, but use it to stand on and the support you thought you had may disappear, and yourself with it. Grab the canister of salt instead of sugar when cooking and the delicious-looking cake will be entirely other than what you expect when you cut it and eat it. I've never forgotten spotting an entry in my rector's calendar thirty years ago in Yorkshire when I was his curate: "Tues. Feb. 18. Fun: 2:30." I wondered what the devil the old boy was up to and was crass enough to ask him. "Funeral: 2:30," he said. No, things are not always what they seem.

A paradox is exactly this: two things placed side by side, apparently in contradiction to each other. Examine the phrases with a little more care and a chink of light appears. What they seem to say together they do not in fact assert separately. A paradox is a powerful literary tool, a clever figure of speech.

St. Paul does not scorn to use literary tools in his writings, and on one remarkable occasion he piles paradox upon paradox seven times when he warms to his theme and thesis.

Yet enough is as good as a feast, so let us apply the first of these paradoxes to Christ and see how it fits. *Imposters who speak the truth.* First you have to remember his desert temptations, and what they were: "*If* you are the son of God." He was being tempted to doubt his integrity as God's Son. Israel of old in the desert had been tempted, and had fallen. Not so, Christ. No sooner does he begin his work in Galilee, than his integrity is challenged, his credentials questioned. Do not be surprised. The claims he makes for what he says are outrageous to the establishment. The established church of his day is soon on to him. He speaks with authority "and not as one of the Scribes." "Who are you to say these things?" "I say so because my Father tells me to say so." His imperturbability maddens the doubters, the accusers. Jesus baffles them, as his miracles and his acceptance by the common people who hear him gladly dismay them. Make no mistake; the claims he makes for what he says leave us at this stage in history exactly where he leaves the establishment of his day. They are either true, or he is a deceiver, a blackguard, a liar, and a cheat. He claims Sonship of God. People challenged that claim then, as they *had* to challenge it, for his claims were not at all recognizably similar with what they thought, or had been taught. Read the Gospels. Read the clashes with the Pharisees and Sadducees. They have an investment in seeking to prove he is an imposter, a liar, for they are high-minded men, they are good men for their time and in their own lights, and they want to preserve the faith they have inherited.

And remember one thing. There are others beside the Pharisees and Sadducees who come to doubt the truth of his claims. His own disciples. They falter at the end, fall apart, run away, lie to save their own skin, not so much from despair at seeing the odds so hopelessly stacked against him, as from the *credibility gap,* too wide for them at the last hours in Jerusalem to leap.

Then there is Pilate. Unwittingly, unwillingly, he discerns that he is to be the arbiter and judge of an internal squabble of the Jewish population in Jerusalem. He is a soldier first, a governor second, in charge of a population with practices he does not share and an outlook he does not care for. He is not there because he is popular with the people or with their leaders, religious pundits with awkward demands who despise him as heartily as he despises them. He is the product of a rough, pagan tradition. The Jewish leaders know his superstitions, his fears, his limitations. They, the council or Sanhedrin, are biblical scholars, academics, and there is friction between "the Separated Ones," the Pharisees, and a group of aristocratic families who supply the High Priesthood with incumbents, the Sadducees, the Holy Ones, sophisticated, loud-talking, assured and worldly, not at all "separated." Together, for some reason, they have realized a common enemy and have asked for military help in arresting him: a troublemaker, a possible insurrectionist. It is this which worries Pilate. It was not so difficult to persuade him to act as he did. There has been an arrest in the Gethsemane Garden and the prisoner has been brought before the council who now bring him to the fortress headquarters, bound, silent, and standing in front of him. For a troublemaker, the man is dignified and alarmingly in control of the situation.

Pilate is puzzled: the charge of sedition he expected has not been made, and Jesus does not look like a revolutionary leader. "You—are *you*—the king of the Jews?" "Is that your own idea, or have others suggested it to you?" The captive Christ is utterly unafraid. Pilate blusters: "What have you done?" Christ's answer is given in the imperturbable claim of kingship: "My kingdom does not belong to this world; if it did, my followers would be fighting to save me from arrest by the Jews." "You are a king, then?" and in so doing he uses a word which the prisoner has not used: the term *king*. Here stands a man who talks of a kingdom, which to Pilate means armies and power and grandeur—and that might mean a threat to Rome. But his kingdom is not of this world. The man is talking nonsense. He is an imposter, a poseur, a deceiver. The prisoner, this imposter, continues: "For this was I born; for this I came into the world, *and all who are not deaf to truth* listen to my voice." If Pilate had stopped at that moment to listen to the answer to his question "What is truth?" he might have heard "I am."

"An imposter who speaks the truth"? So much for Jesus. What about the rest of us? As God's servant I have to be an imposter who speaks the truth. If I bear this mark of the Lord Jesus what will it mean for me? First, it will mean that I shall have to get used to the idea that the secular world will never really understand me and what I am saying. For I can live to the full and enjoy life quite enormously and yet know also that there are eternal values, coming into and governing every aspect of the life I live. It means then that in a peculiar way I shall as a Christian be saying something and meaning something which is slightly different from what others will be saying and meaning. In that way I shall be an imposter who speaks the truth. I meet death in my family, but the way I deal with it, with the approach to it, with the moment when it comes for a loved one, will be different from the way people have to face it who do not really want to find time to deal with God. For my grief, which is very true, very deep, and just as heartfelt, will have joy in it, too—joy, knowing that Christ has, as the Scriptures say, "gone before," tasted death, shackled its powers, and risen again. Therefore because of our prayers for our loved ones who stand on another shore and in a greater light, we are not "sorry as men without hope, for them that sleep in him," and know that they are praying for us, too. But I doubt that the world will understand this way of coping with death.

Suppose someone does me a grievous and great wrong. I am robbed either of reputation or a friendship or a position I had so hoped to have. Someone takes something to which on all counts I am entitled; it is rightfully and justly mine, whatever it is, and I am defrauded of it. I have disappointment, yes. A grievance, yes. Anger perhaps for a short time, or even a fleeting hope for revenge when once I have retrieved what is mine. The worldly world expects this of me, applauds me, cheers me on in my self-justification. I am encouraged to get my rightful desserts. But Christ, the imposter to Pilate who yet speaks the truth, bids me seek vengeance less; to extend his mercy. For he reminds me that vengeance is *his,* not mine to wield: *he* will repay. And when I consider how his vengeance *is* his mercy, not a victory of his better self over his worse self, like mine would be, that his wrath *is* a side of his love that sin cannot approach to sour, that all he does and *is,* is love, and life—then *to extend his mercy, to seek reconciliation in situations where worldy common sense would tell us to strike a blow,* is to the secular world a sham, a play-act, or at the very best an act of folly.

I accept a humiliation—which is after all the only way to learn humility, and this Christ has taught me—and am judged weak-kneed, stupid, dumb, craven. I shall be an imposter. The secular world will not quickly understand. It will never completely understand when as a fallible, frail human being I have to make a tremendous struggle in my fallen conscience to allow meekness, mercy, temperance, and forbearance to have control over me. The secular world will not quite understand my reactions at the slings and arrows of outrageous fortune, such as suffering accepted, pain acknowledged and then transfigured. For the worldly world will be slow to understand transfiguration; much slower even to credit the truth of it, for the dimension in which transfiguration takes place is a dimension unknown and untrustworthy to the man who says he wants it told "where it's at." Tell him where it's *really* at, and he won't believe you. You are an imposter.

As Christians we shall *always* be imposters who speak the truth while we proclaim an allegiance to the unseen, to values eternal as well as temporal, to a man who claims he is God with a birth disputed, a childhood unknown, his sayings discarded, his healings rejected, his resurrection and ascension debated and reduced; his church discredited for its manifest cruelties and ignorances in the centuries since he built it. We shall *always* be imposters who speak the truth so long as we affirm a source of life beyond life, a source of joy beyond the world's assessment of fulfillment and happiness. We shall always be imposters just as long as we own the one who transfigures suffering, who hides us in his wounds, where nothing can separate us from his love.

Whose Life Is It Anyway?

I happen to listen to my radio quite a lot. Apart from the music and the news I frequently and regularly listen to the advertisements, which I like, such as those for Dannon Yogurt, the Look for the Union Label, and how *Time* magazine makes everything more interesting, including you. And then there's that very popular magazine, *Playboy.* The ads of the past few weeks have been concerned to show how its young readers are the up-and-coming "new materialists"; of the *Playboy* reader, "his lust is for life." Admittedly, that phrase is clever: "His lust is for life." At least it doesn't claim that the reader's life is for lust!

"His lust is for life." What sort of life? The sort of life where achievement and success and advancement lie? In love? In possessions? In social esteem? In marriage? In family pleasures and the consolations of the marriage bed? In club memberships? In business prospects and promotions? Perhaps all these, or some. Certainly this sort of life has its hedonistic side. Certainly, this sort of life has its shallow side, its snobbish side, where the "pride of life" can strut. Certainly, this sort of life can bring out the less attractive side of the character, the envious side, the covetous side, the dishonest side, as well as the acquisitive side. Not very nice when you look at it like that—and forget as you "damn with faint praise and assent with civil leer" the legitimate, serious ambitions of a young man who wishes the best for his wife and family, who wants to make sure, as sure as he can, that his responsibilities as husband and father are exercised. His name is Legion. His lust is for life indeed, but it is a life with an extra dimension. And that brings worship out of him as well as work. More of that later.

Our Lord has some uncomfortable words to say about life and the lust for it. "No man is worthy of me who does not take up his cross and walk in my footsteps. By gaining his life a man will lose it" (Matt. 10:38-39a). Those are terrible words. They are capable of inspiring terror, and they are meant to do so. At Passiontide each year, the church's attention is drawn to the sufferings of Christ of which the Via Dolorosa, the trek up the Calvary Hill to Golgotha with the cross on his back, was the penultimate agony. Discipleship involves Christ's indignity, and a person's worthiness is judged by readiness to accept it, knowing that crucifixion is at the end of cross-carrying. Christ does not ask us to carry a cross up to the Place of a Skull in order that it may be there for somebody else to lie and be nailed on. Cross-carrying involves readiness to be crucified, for his footsteps led to a hill and to a shelf on the upright of the cross, and stayed there because they were nailed to it. Cross-carrying was the special humiliation reserved for convicted criminals sentenced to death. It is not a form of light mortification, practiced for a time only and then followed by a period of recuperation to recover from breathlessness, chafing, and bruising. The end of it is death.

Christ is saying in words as plain as possible that the test of discipleship, of worthiness of him, is not so much putting up with annoyances, even grievous ones, not so much being brave at the "slings and arrows of outrageous fortune," but facing what he has to face, where he is facing it, and to go with him to the very end of it. Who is sufficient for these things? Peter thought he was and said so: "Lord, . . . I am ready to go with you to prison and to death" (Luke 22:33). Thomas thought he was and said so: "Let us also go, that we may die with him" (John 11:16). All very heroic with their foolish, grand gestures of courage. There is nothing heroic in *this,* there can be no histrionics because there is nobody to overhear, nobody to applaud, no crowds to cheer us on, no companions whistling and singing among the ranks like the soldiers did in the First World War as they marched through the streets to the trains bound for the battlefronts in France. For this is isolation, this is desolation, this is dereliction, this climb up the hill, to what a friend of mine poetically and powerfully has described as "death, profound death, absolute death, death the blank end."

Jesus approaches us individually and looks into our eyes. He confronts us quietly, with his solitary testing, for he is himself isolated in his suffering, alone, deserted. What he wants to know from us is whose we think our life is. Our own? Lived on our terms? Gained and guarded until something more powerful than ourselves manages to pull it from our clutches in that primeval tug-of-war? Are people in fact "at some time . . . masters of their fates" (Shakespeare's *Julius Caesar*)? Was William Ernest Henley right to contend,

Out of the night that covers me,
Black as the Pit from pole to pole,
I thank whatever gods may be
For my unconquerable soul. . . .

It matters not how strait the gate,
How charged with punishments the scroll,
I am the master of my fate:
I am the captain of my soul.

Was he right? This attitude, on first sight brave and courageous, ministers to our self-sufficiency and leads to the fatal forgetting of who we are and whose we are. It is in fact the lust for life we were thinking of before, the lust which resents the abdication of the personal will and choice in deference to the will of Somebody Else (and God is the Divine Somebody Else); the lust which is uneasy at the thought of what costly sacrifice might involve as a restriction to its activities; the lust for life which sees, for instance, vocation to the religious life and the monastic vows of poverty, chastity, and obedience as "a waste"; the lust which is impatient with spiritual values, spiritually tone deaf. There is, you see, in this lust for life a terror of death, an unwillingness even to think about it, and a desire to disguise it. Bad morticians cater to it when they see it. There was the true story of the lady somewhere on the West Coast who was buried sitting at the wheel of her car—the thing she had loved so much!

In 1974 a member of my congregation died six days after his confirmation, and died on the eve of Advent Sunday, the day when traditionally the church considers the first of the Four Last Things: death itself, the first indeed of the four ultimate issues with which humanity has to contend. Writing a sermon that Saturday was a piercing business, and I wrote it for Richard. In it I referred to this terror of death. I want to continue the examination of it with the remarks I made then in mind.

I think I know just where the terror may lie. It is *the fear of losing control over ourselves.* Our control certainly is never absolute, never complete. We have little control over a sneeze. The philosophers of old used to point to the sneeze as one of the two human activities which reason had no part in or control of. The other is a certain stage in love when rational control over our bodies ceases and nature herself takes over the controls from men and women. Then there is sleep; we can delay it but it is rare that our control over it is complete. Sometimes we are frightened of sleep, of what we may miss, of what may happen while we are in it, of the dreams that may come to us. Sleep is a little death. Death is a situation over which we have no control, except by bringing it upon ourselves.

But this fear of losing control over ourselves is something deep within us all, hidden but still there and disclosing itself in ways we do not expect. Here are three clues. One is being bossy or being driven to dominate. Domination and control over others makes for security against the threatened loss of all control. To insist on living in the past is another; to refuse to see the necessity for coming out of it. There is hardly anything more pathetic than the subterfuge of *mutton dressing as lamb,* when the person refuses to accept the inevitable onset of old age and in looks and dress tries a disguise which fools only himself or herself. The third is something I myself have had to recognize. Perfectionism. One day a priest was watching me straighten out a desk and some bookshelves; everything was put back in its precise place, things were in completely symmetrical order on the desk, and so on. "There is nothing obsessional about you, is there?" he observed sarcastically. That is one of the clues, and I am forced shamefacedly to admit it. My colleagues in the ministry would attest to it, bless them.

But how *not* to fear death? Not by pretending it will never happen. Facing it, facing its solitariness by dying daily, as the Scriptures tell us—this is the hard way, this way of mortification, which is a Latin word meaning "to make to die," or "to make death." Remember that when our Lord talks about the lust for life, it is life lived on one's own terms: "by gaining *his* life a man will lose it." Make peace with the fact that the Lord's life is what he wants us to share in. Willingness to have Christ's life given to us is the willingness to let him do with ours what he wants. It means death to our lesser selves which have been allowed to grow to major proportions. St. Paul knows this: "For his sake I have suffered the loss of all things, and count them as refuse, in order that *I may gain Christ* and be found in him . . . that I may know him and the power of his resurrection, and may share his sufferings, *becoming like him in his death,* that if possible I may attain the resurrection from the dead" (Phil. 3:8ff., RSV). *That* death to the lesser self is the climb uphill with the cross on your back, with humiliation and pain, and the prospect at the end of it, for love of him who would say of all he loves: "A lust for life? My life!"

Promises, Promises

HERE is a serious letter, a crisis letter from a tiny child to God. These letters open great themes of the faith to us and this one a majestic subject. "Dear God, I wrote to you before do you remember? Well, I did what I promised. But you did not send me the horse yet. What about it? Lewis."

"Promises, promises . . ." and little Lewis is next in line in the chorus of those who echo that famous complaint. Moreover he is calling God to account for his failure to honor his side of the bargain: "I wrote to you before do you remember?" Lewis wrote; we think we pray. He wants a horse. He has set his heart upon a horse. He wants that horse more than anything in the world. We have our horses, too: the things, the money, the people, the situations, the power—we want more than anything in the world. The chances are that for Lewis a horse is a pipe dream. Such, alas, are many of the things upon which we have set our hearts, power unavailable to us, situations impossible of fulfillment, people inaccessible to our grasp, money unprocurable, things unattainable. We do not necessarily want them in the worst way, but they form a part of our fantasy lives.

I often say that there is no such thing as pure chance. Things do not merely *happen;* God allows them to happen, allows our feet to tread the paths of their happening. So it came to pass once in Birmingham, Alabama, during some preaching duty, that I spent an afternoon struggling with the soul of a young man I had known merely by letter after replying to some official questions he had written as a seventeen-year-old student during my Lambeth days in the early sixties. It appears that at the university two years previously he had met a girl in the elevator and had fallen in love with her, love so deep that it blinded him to everybody and everything else. Then suddenly she dropped out of college, out of his life, out of the family, and disappeared. "I have thought about nothing else for two years," he said to me. He knew one thing. He had to find her. The fact that she had simply gone, left him and her college life without a word from that day to this was as nothing in his determination to find her. He had sought her sorrowing. He was convinced he would get her back. He was obsessed by this, and he dreamt she was in Birmingham and had driven through the night from a place in Mississippi because of it, convinced he would find her, and would get her back.

The heart has its reasons, we are told. Mrs. Wallis Warfield Simpson, who married the Duke of Windsor, used those words as a title to her book. But the heart's reasons have their own rules. I remember Caryll Houselander's disturbing words in "The Reed of God":

> If ever you have loved anyone very deeply, and then lost him through separation, estrangement, or even by death, you will know that there is an instinct to look for him in every crowd. The human heart is not reasonable; it will go on seeking for those whom it loves even when they are dead. It will miss a beat when someone passes by who bears them the least resemblance; a tilt of the hat, an uneven walk, a note in the voice. (P. 127)

If Lewis had got his horse there was the problem of what to do with it. If my poor young friend had found the person he was seeking, what would the confrontation be like when they met? Lewis had made a bargain with God. In exchange for the desire of his heart he had promised something and he had kept the promise he made. I suspect my young friend had made some such bargain with God. In fact I know he had. He, like Lewis, had tried to harness the Divine power to a heart-wish of his own, and neither was satisfied with the results of his effort, his deal.

Their deal. It is tempting to try to work a deal with God. But it is unsatisfactory because the fire of the Divine love which blazes in the heart of God approaches all our heart-wishes and cauterizes all our motives of will and desire; and does it for our final blessedness. It is all for our good, all for our future companionship with him. Whether we write like Lewis, whether we barnstorm the gates of heaven like John, however we approach the Lord with the things we want most in the world, they have to go through that fire. And then, *and then,* on the other side of that refining fire we meet *God's promises to us.*

And that is a very different story. Most of you will be familiar with the term *New Deal.* President Franklin D. Roosevelt used it in his time as an economic plan. An eminent citizen was asked to comment on the term and he replied that he was not interested so much in a New Deal as in a Fair Deal. Whatever the merits were of the New Deal (and I am certainly not competent to assess them) the term itself *is* interesting. For back along the ages, long before anyone had thought up the name Roosevelt—or America, for that matter—there was a New Deal, and it was a fair deal, a square deal, because the dealer, if I may so express it, was God, and the man he made it with was Noah, after the flood which devastated the land had subsided.

> And God spake unto Noah, and to his sons with him, saying, And I, behold, I *establish my covenant with you,* and with your seed after you; And with every living creature that is with you, of the fowl, of the cattle . . . from all that go out of the ark. . . . Neither shall there any more be a flood to destroy the earth. . . . This is the token of the covenant which I make between me and you . . . for perpetual generations: I do set my bow in the cloud. . . . And I will look upon it, that I may remember the everlasting covenant between God and every living creature of all flesh that is upon the earth.
>
> *Gen. 9:8-16, KJV*

The ancient story of the flood which had destroyed the land was a saga of remarkable spiritual perception of God's disapproval of the way things were going, the way of selfishness which humankind was intent on taking. It told of a cataclysm which devastated all life except that which had been "saved" and was afloat in the ark. First the disapproval, then the destruction, next the reconstruction of relationships between Creator and the created order beginning with man. And then through man extended to every living thing. God, so to speak, wanted to start again, set his creation off on the right track. He initiated a promise, a new deal for humankind. But note these things: (1) God was the initiator, as he always is; (2) the fire of the Divine love in its holiness and judgment had come very close to man's wishes and had purified his aspirations in so doing; (3) *it was not a bargain;* for (4) the terms were God's, as his dealings with us always are. But note that they bound him, for his love set the terms of that covenant, that magnificent promise, and there are no inconsistencies, no contradictions, no conscience clauses in a promise dictated by the loving purpose of a holy God. This new deal was a *promise,* a promise of self-giving, a promise of commitment, a promise of protection, a promise of salvation, no less, to a people and to a creation. All were embraced. The people became the People of the Covenant, forever surrounded, forever encircled with the rainbow of the love of their Creator. *And that covenant, that promise, has never been annulled.*

That is the earliest recorded understanding of the promises of God. From that solemn foundation, other promises followed. God has through history continued to pour himself into the lives of men and women, through prosperity and adversity, through fat years and lean years, through pestilence, famine, exile, and the threat of war. He promises himself, and what greater promise could there ever be than that? And he kept his promise. He gave himself to us in Christ.

St. Paul knew this and expressed it in a remarkable theological nutshell. In his second letter to the church in Corinth he writes: "The Son of God, Christ Jesus, proclaimed among you by us . . . is the Yes pronounced upon God's promises, every one of them. That is why, when we give glory to God, it is through Christ Jesus that we say 'Amen'" (2 Cor. 1:19-20). Christ *is* the promise in its total and dazzling fulfillment, the eternal affirmative proclamation of it, the everlasting Yes.

And he continues to make promises. The difficulty with them is where to begin, for they are many and they are magnificent. They are generous, they are self-giving, but they have *bite.* They have the effect of placing *ours* in a perspective which is sobering to the thoughtful soul for there is no bargaining. I give you twelve. They concern life lived in him. They never minister to our lesser desires.

> Ask, and you will receive; seek, and you will find; knock, and the door will be opened. For everyone who asks receives, he who seeks finds, and to him who knocks, the door will be opened.
>
> *Matt. 7:7-8*

> Here I stand knocking at the door; if anyone hears my voice and opens the door, I will come in and sit down to supper with him and he with me.
>
> *Rev. 3:20*

> Indeed anything you ask *in my name* I will do, so that the Father may be glorified in the Son.
>
> *John 14:13*

> Set your mind upon his kingdom, *and all the rest will come to you as well.*
>
> *Luke 12:31*

> Not everyone who calls me "Lord, Lord" will enter the kingdom of Heaven, *but only those who do the will of my heavenly Father.*
>
> *Matt. 7:21*

> All that the Father gives me will come to me, *and the man who comes to me I will never turn away.*
>
> *John 6:37*

> Whoever seeks to save his life will lose it, and whoever loses it *will save it, and live.*
>
> *Luke 17:33*

> For it is my Father's will that everyone who looks upon the Son and puts his faith in him *shall possess eternal life; and I will raise him up on the last day.*
>
> *John 6:40*

And mark this: *I am sending upon you my Father's promised gift.*

Luke 24:49

And be assured, I am with you always, to the end of time.

Matt. 28:20

Twelve promises; all are true, for his claims are vindicated, his victory won, his life available to us. So nevertheless, "I live, yet not I, for Christ himself liveth in me."

Do you know this little hymn? It is a hymn which perhaps Lewis along with all of us might learn to love.

Lord be thy word my rule,
In it may I rejoice,
Thy glory be my aim,
Thy holy will my choice.

Thy promises my hope,
Thy providence my guard.
Thine arm my strong support,
Thyself my great reward.

Life in the Slow Lane

SOME people live life in the fast lane. They seem to enjoy it, if they can stop long enough to converse with the likes of us who are not in it. But what about those of us who live life in the *slow* lane? What about those for whom life began at a disadvantage? There are many of them, to be sure. What about those who have no help either with brains or looks or background or money or prospects or personality? Life looks as though it will certainly be in the slow lane for them. What started me thinking about this was—as usual—a portion of Scripture from the New Testament: the reaction of the people in Christ's hometown when he began on the Sabbath to teach in the synagogue:

> and the large congregation who heard him were amazed and said, "Where does he get it from?", and, "What wisdom is this that has been given him?", and, "How does he work such miracles? Is not this the carpenter, the son of Mary, the brother of James and Joseph and Judas and Simon? And are not his sisters here with us?" So they fell foul of him. Jesus said to them, "A prophet will always be held in honour except in his home town, and among his kinsmen and family."
>
> *Mark 6:2-4*

The strike against Christ was that he was judged illegitimate. When a man was known by his name to be only the son of a mother, and not with a father's name attached, he was adjudged a bastard. That was the way they spoke, and that was the way it was. Son of Mary, not son of Joseph. His kinsmen and family were no kinder, as he tells us plainly. They resented his teaching and preaching to them, as if he was "better" than they. Yet they could hear his bastardy declared around them and it brought shame to them. He was an albatross around their necks, an embarrassment, amiable but odd, a pretentious talker, a disadvantaged relative, a brother with a strike against him, no credit to them, a nuisance, the bitter cause of gossip and unease.

And that brings to mind another passage of Scripture—this time from the Old Testament, the eleventh chapter of the Book of Judges:

> Jephtha the Gileadite was a great warrior; he was the son of Gilead *by a prostitute*. But Gilead had a wife who bore him several sons, and when they grew up they drove Jephtha away; they said to him, "You have no inheritance in our father's house; you are another woman's son." So Jephtha, to escape his brothers, went away and settled in the land of Tob.
>
> *Judges 11:1-3a*

For Jephtha life too begins at a disadvantage. Born out of wedlock, born from lust and in sin, life promised to be in the slow lane for him, with the strike of illegitimacy against him, and his half-brothers' rejection, too. Imagine the realization that he was not as the others were, that there was a slur on his name, that the children he grew up with in the same house had prior claim to everything and everyone before him. The story goes on to say that he drifted into bad company but that he finally made good, a warrior big in deed and courage, and a man of his word, tragically and sadly so. You might like to read that story. It is a poignant but a triumphant tale.

It was not coincidence that Christ should choose to be born poor. It is not coincidence that he should choose to be born underprivileged and in an occupied nation. It is not coincidence that within that shackled nation he should be born with a slur on his name, born into the slow lane, born with a strike against him even by his own townsfolk and kinsmen, in the words of the prophet Isaiah, "a scorn of man and an outcast of the people." For he was in himself the embodiment and the enfleshment of all that that prophecy of the Suffering Servant could possibly convey—all that, and more. He *is* the meaning of what the Psalmist said when he sang "the stone which the builders rejected has become the chief cornerstone" (Ps. 118:22). The salvation of the world required that he should taste to the bitter dregs the chalice of faulty human judgment against him and all humanity; that he should be for all men the loser in the world's assessment of what wisdom and goodness consist of, in order to overturn the confident assessments of selfish humanity. In this way he was to show the world what life is really all about, in the life of resurrection after death, to come back in the face of all evidence to the contrary to a world which thankfully thought it had seen the last of him. To live out in himself the truth of the ancient claim of God with us:

> My thoughts are not your thoughts, and your ways are not my ways. . . . For as the heavens are higher than the earth, so are my ways higher than your ways, and my thoughts than your thoughts; and as the rain and the snow come down from heaven and do not return until they have watered the earth, making it blossom and bear fruit, and give seed for sowing and bread to eat, so shall the word which comes from my mouth prevail; it shall not return to me fruitless without accomplishing my purpose or succeeding in the task I gave it.
>
> *Isa. 55:8-11*

So Christ the Word of God accomplishes what God wants: the salvation of the world, in ways of wisdom inaccessible to the mind and wisdom of humanity. When he quotes the Scriptures that he had learned as a child for the pattern of his obedient work, he talks only in terms of the disadvantaged, the unfortunate, those with every strike of adverse circumstance against them, condemned to life in the slow lane. He never mentions the choice of the clever, the noble, and the confident and strong for anything: nowhere can be found the promise of crowns to the conquerors, except in the conquest of will and self. For he has come, he says, to preach the gospel to the poor and brokenhearted, to set at liberty the captives and to give light to the blind. Dr. Schuller of the Crystal Cathedral talks about the necessity for a good self-image to receive Christ's offer of salvation. My reading of the gospel persuades me that it is addressed precisely to those for whom a good self-image is denied, the bereft of any form of possession, whether of hope or ideas of self, *whatever,* and if like children we can take that offer unself-consciously or without self-assessment, then it is ours for the asking. "Nothing in my hand I bring; simply to thy Cross I cling."

This should set our perceptions right about who we are and what we are here for and what we have to look forward to. Christians like Christ himself still affirm joy and hope, despite the discouragements which may surround us like bees for a time, and which are nailed on to our backs like his cross. Of course they slow us down in the race of life, and are impediments to what we are tempted to think of as our rightful opportunities for achievement and fulfillment: recognition, justice, or a place in the sun. The hard facts of this life are that there *are* areas of unfulfillment, disappointment, discouragement, to the end of our days. Legislate as wisely as we may, tackle abuses of justice as we try, fight for the things that go to put the world to rights, and some still will travel in the slow lane, remain unfinished as humans, with failure their daily bread, its sour taste their ration on this side of life's river.

But—again—we must look at him in whom the whole paradox of failure and victory are seen, the person in the vortex of human history, who in himself is the measure of our hope: the despised and rejected of men, a man of sorrows and acquainted with grief.

Discouragement was not alien to Christ. Christ knew it. He was not joking when he said, "The Son of Man hath not where to lay his head." He was discouraged when he was a victim of inhospitality. Yet he had been born a victim of inhospitality. He knew rejection. How many times are we told of his discouragement at not being able to perform miracles of healing because of people's unbelief? Or of the opposition and obtuseness of his own kith and kin? Did not his heart sink at the thought of his sufferings which he knew his obedience to the Father would cost him? Did he laugh it off when he had asked his disciples to stay awake as he prayed, only to come and find them all dead to the world, dead to his need, dead to the realization of their destiny? Or when the certainty that he was to be betrayed by someone he loved came to him? Did he wave a breezy goodnight as he watched his disciples duck under the olives into the safe shadows as they forsook him in Gethsemane Garden and fled back into the busy town? Did he nod genially at Peter, swearing away in the High Priest's house in front of the fire, busily denying he had ever known or been with him? No. He knew discouragement and the fatigue of spirit; the "heaviness" which can come with it. He knew it. He knew it to the depths. He had lived with it all his life; his mission misunderstood, his motives impugned, his disciples all experts at getting hold of the wrong end of every stick he offered them; the religion he had learned caricatured by those who taught and practiced it professionally, and it was crowned, yes, crowned on the cross itself, with a ghastly diadem, when the forces of disorder within the universe tried to smother the unique companionship with his Father so that he could cry, "My God, my God, why hast thou forsaken me?"

And yet. And yet! He can through it all make this promise, and faithful souls have lived to sing the truth of it: "*Let not your heart be troubled:* ye believe in God, believe also in me. In my Father's house are many mansions: if it were not so, I would have told you. I go to prepare a place for you" (John 14:1-2, KJV).

And, as if that were not enough, with all he had to bear, he could say, "Come unto me, all of you who are tired of carrying heavy loads, and I will give you rest. Take *my* yoke upon you, and learn from me, because I am gentle and humble-hearted. For my yoke is good to bear, and my load is light" (Matt. 11:28-30). You work with a yoke; you *walk* with a yoke. You don't just stand there. His yoke is for our pilgrimage, with him, to our heavenly Jerusalem, and we shall know that it is good to bear, that

There's no discouragement
Shall make us once relent
Our first avowed intent
To be a pilgrim.

God's Promises To You When Impatient

MOST of us have heard stories of the patience of Job. It is a phrase we often use: the patience of Job. If ever a man were tried and tested by adversity, it was that man. In the first place, he was godly, and the things that happened to him could in no way be thought of as retribution for wrong done; there were no pigeons coming home to roost, he had sown no evil seed, to reap an evil. In the second place, he was rich, and in the Hebrew psychology of his day riches were seen as special blessings conferred by God upon righteousness. That he had to experience the loss of his flocks and herds and possessions including his family (except for his wife who on occasions was to remind him of unpleasant realities) was a deep mystery to the people who were told this story. Furthermore, to lose his health and strength and to be visited by the nastiest and most self-righteous bunch of people later described as his *comforters,* was certainly the most vexing thing of all. Yet he maintained his dignity, deprived of everything that possibly could sustain it, and he trounced his tormentors without resorting to invective. Read the story. It is an extraordinary mosaic of what is called "wisdom literature"; while it is not necessarily easy reading, there is pathos and grandeur and poignancy on its pages. Through it comes the picture of both wounded nobility and naked humanity, and long-suffering in every possible sense of that term. Job asks God why, and God refuses to tell him in the terms which make for easy acceptance or even understanding.

All of us ask "why?" at one time or another in our lives. We say we are owed an explanation. We say we deserve being told. And we resent it when the explanation is not forthcoming. When things happen across our path, to hinder our purpose and our plans, we fret at the frustrations we encounter. I often quote a statement I saw written on a cocktail tray: "Everything in life I like is either illegal, immoral or fattening." We fume at not getting our own way, whether it is with hopes dashed, stratagems spoiled, ploys misfired, plots foiled, partners unresponsive, excuses disbelieved. We are impatient with disappointment and failure; our own, or sometimes (let's face it) with others close to us who experience it. And there is a particular impatience which is very unpleasant: the cold impatience with sickness or weakness on the part of someone we love. When it is the impatience of a cold heart, the impatience which is dredged up from the dry well of a pitiless heart, then it can be sordid indeed, cruel and ruthless, and our judgment will be certain and severe.

You may remember that sordid episode of King David's adultery with Bathsheba, the wife of one of his army captains. Nathan, his chaplain, somehow came to know all about it. So the prophet came to the king and told him the story of the poor man with his own little ewe lamb, sacrificed for an impatient rich man's greed. Do you remember what David said as his anger rose when he heard the tale? "The man deserves to die . . . *because he had no pity.*" That is the impatience I am talking of. It can strike all of us, when we make fists of our hands rather than caress with patient pity.

Then there is the impatience born of arrogance, the impatience of a mind which is genuinely quicker than others, and knows so. It was said of the brave Saint Edmund Campion (the Jesuit who was martyred by us Anglicans on December 1, 1581, after suffering the inhumanities which thirteenth-century kings had devised for rebellious subjects) that "he was a man of excellent parts, though he who rode post to tell him so might come too late to bring him tidings thereof." We have all been made to feel uncomfortable in the presence of people like this, who shine so effortlessly and seem to run so fast. Yet it may do us no harm to reflect upon the unattractiveness of it when *our* impatient pride causes us to be insensitive and overbearing and managing (I am speaking to myself) and superficial and *smart*. I suppose it all comes from a basic lack of trust in the Lord's hold over the world he loves so much and man's primeval urge to put himself in God's place and make himself the center of the universe. We end up self-reliant, independent, fast-talking, and forgetful of whose we are, in our haste affirming who we are. We are made in his image. Remember!

But there is a questing and noble impatience with wrong and injustice and untruth. It makes for crusading souls, it can elicit powers of leadership and valor from a diffident and daunted spirit. Can you remember the horror which struck the poet and artist, William Blake, when he beheld the rape of the English countryside in the Industrial Revolution of the late nineteenth century? His great shout of impatience at its beastliness?

And did those feet in ancient time
Walk upon England's mountains green?
And was the holy Lamb of God
On England's pleasant pastures seen?

And did the Countenance Divine
Shine forth upon our clouded hills?
And was Jerusalem builded here
Among these dark, Satanic Mills?

Bring me my bow of burning gold!
Bring me my arrows of desire!
Bring me my spear! O clouds, unfold!
Bring me my chariot of fire!

I will not cease from mental fight
Nor shall my sword sleep in my hand,
Till we have built Jerusalem
In England's green and pleasant land.

"I will not cease from mental fight"—that kind of noble impatience has to be harnessed properly, aware that if a war is to be won, smaller battles may have to be lost. For there are things like self-sacrifice and "growing up into the measure of the stature of Christ," as Paul says, to consider. These things take time. Christ knows that. He himself recited the psalm a thousand times:

God is king, be the people never so impatient;
He sitteth between the cherubim,
be the earth never so unquiet . . .

And in the Divine serenity the Divine purposes for us and for all humanity are worked out by him with whom a thousand years are as but one day. We are told this plainly, for our comfort, in Psalm 37; first in modern language which is startling and strong to make the point:

Be patient and wait for the Lord to act;
Don't be worried about those who prosper
Or those who succeed in their evil plans . . .

and now in the poetic old translation, the next verses:

fret not thyself, else shalt thou
be moved to do evil. . . .
They that patiently abide the Lord,
those shall inherit the land.

Now. The Scriptures have a lot to say about *abiding*, or "waiting upon God," and when they mention this activity and this attitude they link it with several spiritual benefits: renewal as well as inheriting; salvation, no less. "They who wait for the Lord shall renew their strength, they shall mount up with wings like eagles, they shall run and not be weary, they shall walk and not faint" (Isa. 40:31, RSV).

That this promise to us when impatient has been fulfilled time and again is borne out in a phrase James writes in his letter: "My brothers, whenever you have to face trials of many kinds, count yourselves supremely happy, in the knowledge that such testing of your faith breeds fortitude [patience] and if you give fortitude full play you will go on to complete a balanced character that will fall short in nothing" (James 1:2-4).

I waited patiently for the Lord, and
he inclined unto me, and heard
my calling.

He brought me out of the horrible
pit, out of the mire and clay, and

set my feet upon the rock, and ordered my goings.

And he hath put a new song in my mouth, even a psalm of thanksgiving unto our God.

Ps. 40:1-3

Expecting the Unexpected

ONE of my colleagues has an endearing habit (among many, let it be added) of telling the receptionist in the office entrance at 53d Street as he leaves the church building the initials of his destination. So, out to lunch—OTL.

For months I was at a loss to discover the meaning of an entirely new and other set of initials used not, I hasten to say, by my colleague but by many people in New York. OTB, Off Track Betting. That is the place where people go to place what they are convinced are safe bets. But they would lose their shirts on one bet: that they could predict how God in Christ would behave, for the long story of man's dealings with the mysterious Redeemer and Lord through the centuries has been that he has tried, on the basis of what he has discerned, to expect certain things of God. And when man has been ill-advised enough to place his money, so to speak, on a particular way he could wager that the Lord would behave, he has often lost his bet. Christ *is* "the same yesterday and today and forever"—and yet that sameness hasn't the sameness of something you have already experienced; no, that sameness has the mysterious quality all through it of the *unexpected.*

You can amass evidence about him, but you cannot "contain" him. He is elusive, not because he wants to evade us, but because in the words of Scripture he always has *gone before,* he has beaten us to it. He has always to be caught up with, followed. He is always ahead, waiting for us. The answer to Malcolm Boyd's book of prayers, *Are You Running with Me, Jesus?*, is "No." For he has run ahead and is waiting for us to catch up with him. You can never time him, pace him, place him, nail him. Jacob never said a truer word than when he exclaimed, "Surely the Lord *was* in this place, and I knew it not." Note the word *"was." But he can give himself to you and me, and he does. And that is always how he does it.* That, however, is the end point of these reflections, not the beginning. The point I wish to make is that he is always unexpected.

Of course in some ways he *was* expected. The Jewish world since the days of mighty words of the ancient prophets had been told of the man for whom they were to look. "Behold thy king cometh unto thee, meek and riding upon a donkey." They watched him do just that on the first Palm Sunday. Yes, he was greeted as a king, he was seated as a king, he was treated as a king, that day. And some knew. Not merely his friends knew. Some Pharisees and Scribes who knew the prophecy of Zechariah spotted it when they saw him. But the unexpected thing was that he was not the *sort* of king they had assumed. Isaiah's prophecies had another interpretation when he said:

> *Unto us a child is born*
> *Unto us a son is given:*
> *And the government shall be upon his shoulder:*
> *And his name shall be called Wonderful,*
> *Counsellor, the mighty God, the*
> *Everlasting Father, the Prince of Peace.*
> *Of the increase of his government and peace*
> *there shall be no end.*
>
> *Isa. 9:6-7a KJV*

They assumed a mighty vindication of the wrongs this nation had suffered at the hands of godless conquerors. *Savior* meant something very different. The nation waited for the "day of the Lord" when this would happen. And when John the Baptist, the voice in the wilderness, proclaimed, "Prepare ye the way of the Lord, make straight in the desert a highway for your God!" they took the Lord's nearness to mean an end of Roman power and Greek pagan notions which had infiltrated into the very things that held the nation together and gave it identity and purpose—its religious purity. The hope of his coming kept them going.

And yet, the fact is that when he did come, they did not know it; and they did not know it because he was not the Christ they expected. They expected him to come with a crash of circumstances: a colorful, thrilling, stirring arrival that would rally the nation. But he did not. He turned up in a godforsaken part of the hinterland, in the middle of a census—born right in the middle of a specified *humiliation*—when the hated Romans were writing all their names in census books on lists. He was born at a moment of peculiar misery and resentment. Nothing glorious at all. So he was unexpected in the time of his birth, the place of his birth, the circumstances of his birth—to an unknown girl with a question mark against her name—and although the Gospel records his lineage from King David the fact was that far from his royalty being recognized he was regarded as a bastard, and called such—though possibly you did not realize it—by having his mother's name tacked on to his own, which meant the people knew he didn't have a father. Had you realized that? Well, that is what happened; and you can check it up in the Gospel for yourself if you want to. So he was unexpected *in that*—of all things!

Listen to Dr. Ted Ferris, that wonderful preacher and friend, develop this theme:

> They expected a Christ who would liberate them from Rome. He did not. He liberated them from Satan; from sin and from guilt. They expected a Christ who would dazzle them by miraculous feats. He did not. He healed the sick and he fed the hungry; but he didn't jump off the temple just to dazzle them into belief. He refused to do that.
>
> What is more, they expected a Christ who would instill in the young a love of the *Law*—the Law with a capital L because it was the Law of God that Moses had given them and it covered every aspect of life with rules and regulations, both ceremonial and moral. People were neglecting it, and they were expecting a Christ who would rekindle the love of the law with a capital L. He didn't. He talked about the Law of Love, which was quite different. He said that love is the fulfilling of all the laws.
>
> They expected a Christ who would make life easier. He did not. If anything he made it harder. He talked about crosses, not

crowns. It is harder, infinitely harder, to change yourself than to change your surroundings. I am not saying that it is not important to change the surroundings of other people from time to time, for it is; but the essential thing is to change the person, and it is much easier to change the surroundings in which a person lives than to change the person who lives in those surroundings.

Above everything else, they expected a Christ who would be a smashing success. He was not; he was a dismal failure. They expected a Christ that they could keep to themselves as a nation. They could not. He was like a river, the current of which is so strong that no bank can contain it. They expected a Christ who would promise a happy ending. Everybody likes happy endings. He did not promise the kind of a happy ending that all people really long for. He never let them forget about the girls who might have gone to the wedding, but did not because they were too late, and the man who missed the dinner because he was too busy to accept the invitation. He never let people forget the fact that the door can be closed, and that it can be closed forever; that there is the possibility of missing the bus.

They did not expect anything like that; only a few of the most perceptive ones could see the possibility of a Christ born in a manger and crucified on a cross. So it is no wonder that they hardly recognized him, because he was not the Christ they expected. They were not ready for the Unexpected Christ.

(Theodore Parker Ferris, *Selected Sermons*
[Trinity Church, Boston, 1976], pp. 85-86)

And when he came to die they were not expecting the Messiah to die like that. Like a criminal; like a failure; like a visionary; sold for a cheap price; sold, as we say, down the river. The bankruptcy of his cause was evident: evident to his followers, evident to his enemies. No, for a nation which was expecting the wrong thing, their Messiah could not be expected to fail like that. And then the first Easter Day, as Mary Magdalene wept for her Lord in the garden, and the gardener appeared—or so she thought. Only when he called her name in the way she instinctively knew was his and no other did she recognize the Lord, risen, alive. But in this he was unexpected, too. She recognized him by the name he called her. We are given to understand that but for this she might have long mistaken him. And we are also given to understand that she neither expected him nor expected him to look the way he did.

And this unexpectedness is carried to the Emmaus Road, where two disciples in grief were walking and were joined by a stranger. Yet this stranger as they walked expounded to them, foolish and slow of heart that they were, from the prophets the truth about the work and death and the final vindication of the Son of God. It was as they ate together later that he made himself known to them, "made himself known unto them in the breaking of the bread," as the lovely phrase describes it. Against any possible expectation he made use of *that* occasion to do it and yet, curiously, it was the very occasion when he should do it; because it was on *that* occasion, supremely, that he promised to give himself, those few hours before, in the upper room, at supper with them.

So the unexpected Christ came to those who loved him. And still he comes to hearts whose love for him "will burn within them" with the expectation that he will, though not in the ways they think he will. "For my ways are not your ways, nor your thoughts my thoughts," saith the Lord of Hosts. So beware of Off Track Betting—certainly when you are dealing with the living God.

The Dangers of Getting on Someone's Back

PEOPLE are capable of doing dirty things to one another. Sometimes it takes a brutal form of courage to do the dirty deed. One of the dirtiest is what Eric Milner White, the old saintly Dean of York Minster, used to call "the dishonest honesty of frankness meant to hurt." That sort of frankness which leaves a person wounded and the situation unhelped needs to be nailed for the misery it causes. We need show it no mercy, and we are right to give it no houseroom. It is beastly and cowardly.

But there is such a thing as sharp initial comment addressed to a nation, to a church; comment which comes from a heart concerned *beyond* the issues which provoke the initial criticism, and here we leave room for prophecy. This is something very different, as different as night from day. I don't want to get ahead of myself in telling you this. All I want to do at this stage is to outline the possibility of righteous criticism and denunciation and righteous anger. There *is* such a thing as righteous anger, but it is like a Brahma bull, very tough riding on an uncertain hump; a very dangerous and difficult thing to manage. Our Blessed Lord showed it as the fulfillment in himself of all prophecy, and he wielded it mightily in his righteousness and knowledge of his Father's ways.

But it was too much for the church of his day and the people of his generation. It always is. I think of someone in the lifetime of most of us, George Bell, the English Bishop of Chichester; and at one time one of my predecessors as chaplain to Archbishop Randall Davidson of Canterbury. He was an outspoken critic of the policy of the obliteration-bombing of German cities on the grounds that it was deeply un-Christian. George Bell was not merely brave; he was clever. So clever in fact that he might have succeeded William Temple as Archbishop of Canterbury but for Winston Churchill's refusal to submit his name to the king. Bell was not chosen because Churchill disliked what he had said about obliteration-bombing. The House of Lords, of which he was a member, as are all of the senior bishops, disliked what he said; and it ended up that many Englishmen disliked what he said. What he said was roughly and simply this: that statesmen and rulers have the duty before God to consider the morality of their decisions in every realm of government, and that there are bad weapons, unjust weapons, unrighteous weapons in a struggle in which innocent people and powerless people can needlessly be hurt. Well, we were fighting for our lives, and Winston Churchill's single-mindedness, for which we thank God as a nation, was impatient of moral niceties at that time. So the protestor for righteousness, who made the government uncomfortable, was silenced by being passed over in favor of a more congenial soul, Geoffrey Fisher, as archbishop.

I don't know if you realize that when the English nation gathered after the struggle with Argentina over the Falkland Islands the present archbishop, Robert Runcie, was berated by the Tory government under Mrs. Thatcher for referring to the loss and bereavement experienced on *both* sides by families of the soldiers in the struggle. Some sneer at him yet. Others have used their rejection of his reminder as their rationalization for repudiating his spiritual authority over the church of which they claim to be members, and want to be thought of as loyal members.

Think back. Recall the disturbers of our peace. You will agree that the voice lifted in protest is a voice that many do not welcome, that many would prefer to be silenced and smothered. People do not always like to be reminded, they do not relish having their consciences pricked. The human soul resents intrusion, unasked, unannounced. This is no contemporary phenomenon. It has been the experience of civilization since first it could write what it felt. But you know, there are times in the life of every nation or of every city when it is important that a clear voice speaking true and unpalatable things should be raised and listened to. The possessor of that voice was in the old times called a prophet. He did not always foretell what was to happen; he was not necessarily a forecaster. We know enough about forecasters and our weather to realize how mistaken forecasters can often be.

No, a prophet would look at the pattern of contemporary events. He looked at what the government's policies were; he looked at what the defense plans were; he looked at the field of military operations. He listened to what the councillors were saying at the town hall. He looked to see what effect their words had on the people. He listened to what the church was saying; he looked to see what it did after it said what it had said. In other words, the prophet looked to see if the church practiced what it preached. He looked for integrity in the nation's leaders; he looked at the kind of encouragement they were dispensing to the people. In fact, he felt the nation's pulse. But he did not speak until "the hand of the Lord was laid upon" him. Whether this was a hypnotic trance he went into, we are not sure. But when that hand was laid, then he spoke. And there was no mistaking what he said, no mistaking, that is, unless one had the will and wish to do so. And there was plenty of room for resentment.

And so among the Old Testament literature we have remarkable examples of courageous and clear thinking—remonstrations, warnings of God's anger, encouragement to hope, exhortation to work, to build, to plant, to prune; to remember God. The extraordinary and mysterious thing is that the words of the prophets of old which were, at the time they were expressed, concerned with a particular issue, a particular enemy, a particular offense, a particular policy, a particular victory, a particular hope of that day, can be interpreted rightly and validly used in this, our day. In that way, they are eternal, in that way they are *inspired.* And they are often couched in language of poignant and everlasting beauty, so that souls have caught the flame of their inspiration in later ages, in different times; caught it, and have made the truth of the ancient words flash with contemporary fire and force to persuade and convict and turn the people of their generation and time.

But the source of this inspiration? Certainly the Holy Spirit;

and these prophets have spoken with the power of her wind and breath not necessarily and merely after living *among* the issues of the day, immersed in them and involved in them, but disturbingly often *apart* from them; in deserts and on hillsides in isolation; in contemplating silently and privately and in solitude, gaining perspective from the silence, from being alone, perhaps lonely, apart from being consciously alone with God. This instinct, to withdraw for a time, to enter as it were the inner room in oneself while preparing for the ministry of prophecy, is still with us in the church, thank God, in places so sensibly located as Nashotah House Theological Seminary, tucked away in the farmlands of Wisconsin, where near its lake men and women prepare for the ministry of priesthood and then go into the cities to practice it. Many English priests could likewise testify to the benefit of a seminary education tucked away in the countryside of an old Oxford village. I can testify to the sensibleness of quiet and waiting and *hiding* at that time in one's life when the strongest urge is for involvement and action and experience and accomplishment.

The prophet realized this almost without articulating it, and it gave his words a balance, a perspective, and that sharp cutting edge of the sword of truth, which sooner or later was to anger the complacent and to embarrass the false prophets who cried "Peace, peace" when there was no peace. But that needs courage, too. You recall Nathan's extraordinary frankness with King David and the terrifying denunciation after the story of the poor man who had one ewe lamb. You may remember how Nebuchadnezzar threw the three prophets into the furnace after they had spoken so bravely for God. You may remember Daniel, thrown into the lions' den for persisting in maintaining his religious practices, which offended his fellow officials, and for publically saying so. Do you know that Jeremiah was thrown into a cess pit? Truth so spoken is a costly commodity, and the purveyor of it suffers, and can suffer, martyrdom.

And so to this day. In the past decade Janana Luum, Archbishop of Uganda, met death at the hands of Idi Amin himself, who shot him through the head for persisting in calling a Christian spade a spade. So it was within two decades that someone silenced Martin Luther King, Jr.; and who can tell what the fate of Archbishop Desmond Tutu of Capetown might be?

One of the glories of St. Thomas Church is the series of statues and effigies of those whose witness and proclamation have been baptized in their own blood, with Martin Luther King's memorial in a niche of the wall facing Fifth Avenue. Standing preeminent among this "cloud of witnesses" is John the Baptist, the cousin and herald of Christ. That voice of his shattered and shook the world of his day, the little world of Palestine, as he wandered in his animal skins, accusing and disturbing the complacency and the settled priorities of the people in power. For some at the very top his mention of corruption cut too close for comfort. My first boss, the old rector of Redcar, used to say that a man's soul would be in trouble primarily over two things: sex and shekels. In the case of Herod the King's family it was sex and John nailed the trouble. They could stand his voice no longer and at Herod's command he was martyred. Even in death he was mocked and ridiculed, his severed head on a tray used as a feature in a gruesome dance. John the Baptist had not been involved in causes from his youth up. He had been a child of the desert in its silence and desolation, and it was then that the word had come to him: not in the shriek and clamor of political wrangle. That still small voice of God had spoken to his waiting soul. The Spirit had lit her fire in John's heart. His uplifted voice had shouted God's warnings: wrath to come; nowhere to hide; nothing to claim as exemption from accountability; the need to turn, to be clean, to be ready, ready for the man on his heels, far greater than himself, ready to greet the Messiah with lives turned, washed, cleansed, penitent, the Messiah who had the last word, here and hereafter. Uncomfortable, yes. Unwelcome, yes. Indispensable, yes. Unanswerable, yes.

We need John and people like him. And by God's providence, you mark my words, we shall be given them; to get up our shirts, to get on our backs, to dog our steps, to keep us honest, to keep us mindful. They are the keepers of the conscience of the church and they will never be thanked, for prejudice is precious to most and DO NOT DISTURB is a notice on most front doors. St. Paul puts it right there for all of us when he says "Be not deceived; God is not mocked: for whatsoever a man soweth, that shall he also reap" (Gal. 6:7, KJV)!

Waiting upon the Lord

TALK about prayer and you talk about a possible disaster area for some, a potential danger area for most people. Prayer is a risky business. You are in a territory not your own. You engage in an activity with rules hidden because your Partner in this activity, whose identity is entirely different from what you can imagine, remains hidden; and the rules are made by your Partner, not you. Furthermore, this activity embraces more of what you are than you suspect. Prayer is a struggle with God: to find God's ways, to find why he does the things he does and says the things he says to others and with others, to us and with us. It is also a struggle with the human predicament, our humanity's fallenness, our self-caused inadequacies—why we do the things we do and say the things we say. It is a wrestling match with God. Let me tell you of the classical account: Jacob wrestling with the angel. This is what I mean by prayer being a risky business.

> And Jacob was left alone; and there wrestled a man with him until the breaking of the day. And when he saw that he prevailed not against him, he touched the hollow of his thigh; and the hollow of Jacob's thigh was out of joint, as he wrestled with him. And he said, "Let me go, for the day breaketh." And he said, "I will not let thee go, except thou bless me." And he said unto him, "What is thy name?" And he said, "Jacob." And he said, "Thy name shall be called no more Jacob, but Israel: for as a prince hast thou power with God and with men, and hast prevailed." And Jacob asked him, and said, "Tell me, I pray thee, thy name." And he said, "Wherefore is it that thou dost ask after my name?" And he

> blessed him there. And Jacob called the name of the place Peniel: for I have seen God face to face, and my life is preserved.
>
> *(Gen. 32:24-30) KJV*

In the first place, you are on your own. Prayer is a one-to-One activity. If you listened to that story carefully you will have noticed that Jacob sent his family ahead. He had to be alone with his conscience. You may have to be alone with yours, alone with your anxiety, alone with the preoccupation, whatever it is, glorious or gloomy, that drives you to this one-to-One encounter and struggle. No one can be of help at that moment. Alone, completely alone, Jacob faces his experience. It is scary. It is unpleasant for him. It exhausts his strength. It hurts him. And it lasts all night, when night hours never seem to end and the darkness adds its own sinister dimension to the unknown.

That is the setting, and these are the problems: dryness and stagnation in prayer. The first of four possible clues to dryness and stagnation is the experience of the absence of God. Somehow and sometimes he is not to be located, contacted. There is, as you can see, the beginning of a tremendous frustration in struggling with someone unwilling to be recognized. Remember the story. Jacob grunts as he wrestles: "Tell me, I pray thee, thy name." And God says, "Wherefore is it that thou dost ask after my name?" The language of the ancient story catches the unwillingness of God to make himself known on any other terms than his own. A great master of the prayer-life, Anthony Bloom, a Russian Orthodox archbishop living in England, attests to this phenomenon of the absence of God. Too often and too blithely we assume that whatever our unpreparedness for the encounter, God, who is everywhere, cannot wait to make himself available to us in the way we want: usually by giving us something we think we should have. But the God who hides himself, hides himself only in order to make himself known at times and in situations *he* chooses. We blunder into his presence ill-prepared, with egg of one kind or another on our faces, discouraged, aggrieved, and resentful if, after our ill-planned wrestling, we become aware that we have somehow missed the heart of the encounter. This accounts for much of the disappointment and sense of opportunity lost on the part of those who have presumed that they *need not wait*. The wrestling, you see, needs a good deal of "hanging in there," as we say, watching, waiting, empty of surging and clamant agendas with which to confront the hidden God. "They who wait for the Lord shall renew their strength." That biblical observation is very true. To hang in there, to wait, as the wrestling takes the form of a lengthy grip, is to give God the opportunity to provide you with the strength you need for a good long look. Jacob had that experience with God: "I have seen God face to face."

Second, dryness and stagnation in prayer can come as a result closely allied to the first cause, ill-preparedness: it can come as a result of expecting wrong answers. People normally pray when "other helpers fail; and comforts flee," as the hymn says. They pray when a difficulty in their lives is seemingly insoluble by human ingenuity and incapable of being contained by human wisdom. They pray using God as a celestial lightning conductor, somehow deflecting defeat or disaster or calamity from a given situation in which they find themselves or their loved ones. The prayer as often as not takes the form of a bargain. "If you get me and my loved one out of this, I or we will do thus and so." This is expecting a wrong answer. The prayer as often as not takes the form of a request, with the hope that the answer will be what we want it to be. We forget that "No" is an answer, and God often says it. But in our forgetting we give way to outrage, umbrage, and resentment: what we think is the decent thing for God to do for us goes undone. The Psalms have many references to God being deaf, or asleep, impervious to the cries for solutions to predicaments and disasters. We need to realize that the Divine love is for our final blessedness, and that the will of God has two sides to it, neither in opposition to the other; the permissive and the perfect will of God. The *permissive* will is what God allows us to experience, allows us to be, and the *perfect* will is what he wants us to do with what he allows us to experience and to be. To pray is to struggle and wrestle with this perfect will, from our posture of being instruments of his permissive will. To forget this is to court the certainty of dryness and stagnation in our praying.

A third cause is, surprisingly, fatigue. We tend to do our praying at times when we are not at our best. Some people are morning people. If you are, do not leave your prayers until you are dazed with fatigue in your low point of the day. Try them in the morning and give them the same vigor you reserve for the mental and physical tasks you keep for your best time in the day. I am forever saying to people who come to me for confession that it is when we are at our low ebb physically, when we are fatigued and tired, the resilience against temptation to sin is also at its lowest; we fall usually when our resistance is low. The same thing with prayer; do not assume that God prefers to hear you at 7:30 in the morning when that is the time you are likely to snap at your wife or kick the cat or resent getting out of bed. A tired prayer may be the only thing we can offer, and rather that than nothing. Yet prayer continually offered against our natural grain of performance because of the metabolism we have may dull and dry the capacity to express prayer at all. Here let me add that the making of a prayer rule should not be too ambitious: if you plan to pray for particular people and particular causes, with thanks or with concern, keep that list pruned and keep it fresh. It can become a matter of pride to add to the lists until they are unwieldy in length and lack the sharpness and attention we desire. You are reduced to saying with your list like a Manhattan telephone directory: "Lord, look after all these people I've got my hand over." Keep those lists pruned; keep them fresh; and make sure there's a challenge in them: a cause you are uncertain about, or the name of someone you simply cannot stand the sight of who is your perpetual hair shirt, the bane of your life. Equally it may be an event you do not really want to remember but which may be teaching you something ("It is good for me that I have been in trouble, that therein I might learn thy commandments," is one such prayer offered by a wiser but rueful Psalmist). Keep your lists long, keep them unpruned, keep them cozy, and keep them for a time which may be convenient but when you are not at your brightest and best and you are courting stagnation.

Finally, and this is the most devastating of all: dryness and stagnation in prayer can come from a persistent unwillingness to come to terms with something in one's own character which holds you back from "growing into the measure of the stature of the fullness of Christ." We are required to pay attention to self-examination of motive. In other words, we are required to be penitent. If there is something we need to tackle in our own souls—a relationship which needs to be examined; a complacency about despising somebody or some institution or some ethnic group; our unending blindness about a lack of generosity masquerading as prudence; a rationalizing about anger or rage or resentment which may be irrational, or a compulsion to gossip or to criticize—then until we come to terms honestly with ourselves and humbly seek to amend our lives in this particular way, we must expect our prayer-life to be crippled, dry, stagnant. This is a real problem for a Christian.

Why for a Christian? We are meant to pray, to engage in that wrestling match with God. What emerges from this experience is a discovery about God. You remember the story about Jacob? Jacob "prevailed": he won. We are meant to win. We are meant to learn something from the Lord who wishes to make himself known, but on his terms. Struggling with Christ the Word of God is what makes good people good theologians. The process is the same. "Tell me, I pray thee, thy name—who you are, so that I may know why you do the things you do." "I will not let thee go except thou bless me." "And he blessed him there." And Jacob said, "I have seen God face to face."

Signs of Contradiction

THERE are maddening people in this life who like to provide a proverb for every eventuality. They have a helpful saying for every situation. So they end up by contradicting themselves. "Look before you leap," they will warn in a moment when commitment is necessary. But it is not long before they turn around and declare in the next breath: "He who hesitates is lost." Loftily, they will quote Scripture, perhaps not knowing it is Scripture when something turns out well: "Cast thy bread upon the waters." But shortly afterward they will remind you that "Charity begins at home." They will warm up to a romantic possibility and encourage you: "Faint heart never won fair lady." And then declare moments later that "Discretion is the better part of valor." When finance is discussed, they will caution, "Take care of the pennies and the pounds will take care of themselves," and forget that they have within the same day urged, "In for a penny, in for a pound!" Thus they skillfully negotiate life's obstacles, and leave the rest of us with a curious sense of lost opportunity.

But perhaps a little later, after reflection, you get the paradox. Life is a seeming contradiction in itself. Paul was not without a certain facility with words and paradoxes. But then he is a lawyer! He is a classicist. He is a theologian. He does not scorn to use literary tools in his writing. So when he wishes to describe the servant of God he teases us with a further paradox. The servants of God are *"The unknown men whom all men know."* These words are written not merely *for* us all, but *to* us all, because they can first and foremost refer to Christ himself as God's servant. My suspicion is that subconsciously, if not consciously, Paul had Christ on his mind when he penned this crisp paradox.

Now if any man is Christ-centered, Paul is, and how other could he be with a life stopped in its tracks and diverted so powerfully into Christ's track on that road to Damascus? Let us try to unwrap this paradox and seeming contradiction.

St. Mark sets great store in emphasizing the truth of the *first* part of the phrase when he tells how Christ wanted to preserve what has since come to be known as the *Messianic Secret;* to preserve his anonymity, his unknown-ness, he began his ministry in the towns and villages of Galilee. He well knew that his ministry drew its authority from his unique divine sonship to God. Yet he demanded secrecy from his disciples, because he knew that it was not yet time to become the man all men knew, for all men were not yet ready to understand, to take in, the true notion of what the Messiah was. He demands secrecy. But he did not always get it from those who were not his disciples. Yes, therefore it is the strong affirmation by Christ to be "unknown." And not without cause.

"For he cured so many that sick people of all kinds came crowding in upon him to touch him. The unclean spirits too, when they saw him, would fall at his feet and cry aloud, 'You are the Son of God'; *but he insisted that they should not make him known*" (Mark 3:11-12); and yet—to a man he had healed of a mental illness Jesus said, "'Go home to your own folk and tell them what the Lord in his mercy has done for you.' The man went off and spread the news in the Ten Towns of all that Jesus had done for him" (Mark 5:19-20). And again just after he had raised Jairus's daughter from death, *"he gave them strict orders to let no one hear about it"* (Mark 5:43). After feeding the five thousand he went to Gennessaret, where "he was immediately recognized; and the people scoured that whole countryside and brought the sick on stretchers to any place *where he was reported to be*" (Mark 6:54-55). So, Christ the unknown and disregarded.

The unknown man, known to all men, who charged the faithful to keep his secret—told them to tell the towns what the Lord had done. Christ, the child born in obscurity—yet known to wise men from the East; brought up in a tiny village—yet listened to by the professional theologians on his boyhood pilgrimage to the temple, because of the authority of his inner consciousness of being in the flesh the Son of God. And Christ, the carpenter's strange son, riding on a donkey amid the crowds' excitement into Jerusalem to die. His early life unknown. His temptations, virtually unknown. His young manhood, unknown. His private prayer-life, almost unknown. His death on a cross merely one of three that day. How many had there been on crosses the previous day, or the day before that? So even his death unknown.

And yet well known. For had not the whole city been moved by his triumphal entry some days before, and had not the priests complained that he was upsetting all the people? This obscure young man's name was nevertheless on people's lips even when they were assembling for the Passover, and there was a crowd in the Garden of Gethsemane where the police arrested him to bring him before them.

But it is in the trial before Caiaphas that we see the climax and absurdity of this paradox. Jesus is brought to Caiaphas, the son-in-law of Annas. The whole council—chief priests, lawyers, scribes—are assembled for this ecclesiastical trial. It is an appalling travesty of justice. False evidence is produced, and witnesses give evidence which contradicts. Nevertheless, Caiaphas presses on compulsively: "By the living God I charge you to tell us: Are you the Messiah, the Son of God?" And to that question Christ's answer comes in words everybody knew, words engraven on every heart who heard them, the words used by God to Moses; the words that form the very name of God himself: "I AM." Unknown, and yet the description of himself was well known by every Jew in the world. That is the obscure Galilean who claims he is the Son of God.

"The unknown men whom all men know." But the paradox goes further and is intended to involve us. There is an unknown side of you. It is not necessarily your murky side, your shameful side, the side you would not want your family, much less your friends, to know about. It is not your secret meannesses, your hidden resentments, your personal, irrational rages and hatreds; it is not your unpleasant habits, your private sexual preferences or deviations or activities, your kinks, your kicks, or whatever it might be which you would hate the people who work or live with you to know about. Of course all this is your unknown side—though it is often and surprisingly not so deeply hidden and cunningly concealed as you might think.

No. There is another unknown side of you, infinitely greater, immeasurably better, inestimably more encouraging. It is that part of you which has on perhaps very rare occasions and at no little surprise to yourself encountered another dimension, been brought up against forces mysteriously greater than anything you would imagine a human being would have to meet; an awareness of the reality of spiritual things and values; a discovery that there has been guidance from some source beyond, far beyond your own wisdom and experience. It is an awesome discovery and you have realized that after all there *is* a purpose and a plan and that you are part of it. It may have come at a time of fear or grief, when it seemed that through that dark night of doubt and sorrow strange comfort, strong help was given to you. "Surely God was in this place, and I knew it not," you could say with old Jacob—and there were certainly two sides to him! You have in fact been brought very near to God on those occasions; and that discovery, that recognition, that awareness, *was meant for you alone*. That is your share—and there may be more along the way—of spiritual consolation. You are grateful for it, certainly, surprised at it perhaps, and strengthened by it, certainly. But it is all part and parcel of your secret life with God: your own treasure, hidden at the bottom of the well of your spiritual life. And deep as it is, almost out of sight because it is buried so deep within the secret wellsprings of your heart, it is your real life, *the strongest part of you, hid with Christ in God.* You may indeed be a miserable sinner but you do have this priceless gift—the capacity to want to love God, the naked longing of the soul for companionship with God. Christ knew it, understood it, spoke of it in the Sermon on the Mount: "When you pray, go into a room by yourself, *shut the door,* and pray to your Father who is *there in the secret* place" (Matt. 6:6).

Now to be an effective servant of God I have to make frequent use of this secret place. So let us speak of it and share it. It is my love life with God; it becomes my prayer-life. People call it the *in-*

terior castle. And the castle is not built spectacularly. It is slow, painstaking, humble work. It is secret work, done behind that closed door of which Jesus so often speaks. It is the steady, frank act of the will to build on the foundations of the capacity for loving God. It is a secret pact, unspoken except in the love-whispers made to God. It is the strongest part of us because it is our best part, our humblest part. No one knows it, no one can know it. In this we are *unknown:* we are the unknown men, for we carry in our hearts a secret treasure house, and it gives us strength and balance to be well known in our work and witness. There is no need to wear our heart on our sleeve. Still less need is there for us to badger and hector our fellowmen wherever we meet them with that embarrassing and insensitive kind of witness-bearing which is pompous, self-conscious, and absolutely ghastly, not to say spiritually arrogant: "Are you saved?" Curious it is that the stronger our interior castle the more unself-conscious is our possession of it. Called as all of us are to be saints, we respond to this calling from the *ground of the heart*. But we respond to it—or in our best moments we try to respond to it, and it is in this trying that we *cannot help* being well known.

The late Canon Douglas Webster, formerly a canon of St. Paul's in London and a frequent preacher at St. Thomas, said these words from the pulpit here in 1973:

> You can see an idol. You cannot see the living God. There is a divine restraint and reticence. He hides himself because the sight of him would be too much, too dazzling. He does not want to overwhelm or compel. He is not on show. He is not to be observed, nor will he have his existence proved. We can know him only because he chooses to make himself known to all who have the disposition to consider him, the desire to find him. So the prophet said, "Seek ye the Lord while he may be found; call upon him while he is near." And Jesus said, "Ask and it shall be given you, seek and you shall find, knock and it shall be opened to you." We set off on the pilgrimage, but it is he who invites us and beckons us toward himself. Knowing God means saying yes to him, responding to him in every situation where he makes himself known. If we keep

> He is a God who hides himself because he is unspeakable holiness, inscrutable mystery, a consuming fire of love. But he hides in places and persons where he may be found. For some he hides in a chord of music or a line of poetry, in a painting or a sunset. For some he hides in a friend or neighbor, a cup of cold water, an act of kindness or someone belonging to another race. He hides in a piece of bread and the wine outpoured. Supremely and for everyone he hides in a baby in a manger and a man dying on a cross. He hides not in order to obscure himself but to avoid being misunderstood. He hides because only he who hides can make himself known.

So Christians are a walking paradox—an infuriating contradiction. We are imposters who speak the truth just so long as we claim allegiance to the unseen, to values spiritual rather than relevant and expedient, and we cannot help being known for that. Not that we want for a minute to be thought *better;* all we want to be known for is that we are conscious of being forgiven by a forgiveness greater than we can muster; of being loved by a love which makes the worldly assessment of it look sick and pale; of being upheld by a power which can help us transfigure our suffering and our grief and show us where true joys are to be found; to have a friend whose friendship binds us and liberates us *because* the relationship is so strong and so demanding.

A double life for the Christian then? Not really. Christ's life was a masterpiece of oneness. He claimed: "My Father and I are one," and in him the divine and the human sang together, because they were together. Our job is to grow to the measure of "the stature of the fullness of Christ," as imposters who speak the truth, unknown and yet well known.

There's None So Blind . . .

I had the good fortune to know slightly a legendary woman in Britain. All this century, until she died last year, she captivated and convulsed and scandalized and enslaved both men and women by her astonishing beauty, which she managed to combine with an extraordinary honesty and wit. She was utterly refreshing, alarmingly unpredictable, and had one vanity—shortsightedness, which she never advertised with glasses or contact lenses. So her glorious face would turn blankly right at you until by something you said or a gesture familiar to her she had pinned your identity or located your exact whereabouts. There was a horrifying occasion which she told against herself: at a grand diplomatic reception a quietly spoken woman turned to her and talked of this and that. Something in the voice warned my friend. She realized she was talking to the queen and swept into a deep curtsey, saying as she did so, "Do forgive me, please, Ma'am! I didn't recognize you without your crown on." What the queen replied is not recorded.

Recognition can come as a shock, glad or unpleasant. One of the great barriers to recognition is the habit we all have of a preconceived notion about someone. In our mind's eye, she may be tall. So we are predisposed to consider tall women, and then this small woman comes into view, we are not ready, and recognition is delayed, perhaps disastrously. I saw a poignant sketch in a review some years ago of a young sailor who had been getting letters from a woman. She had written faithfully and he had built in his mind's eye this picture of a pretty young thing. They had agreed to meet. She would be carrying a flower, and sitting on a certain bench in a park they both knew. A little old lady, carrying a flower, came and sat on one end of the park bench. The young sailor appeared and sat on the other. The lady held her flower high. The sailor glanced, but looked away, then got up and left. He left the unrecognized writer of those letters crushed and alone. He had not recognized her. Perhaps he was the one who was really blind.

People run into this difficulty with Jesus. He asks his disciples, "Who do people say I am?" People, his own brothers included, fail to recognize his messiahship. There are lots of conjectures. If he does not observe the Sabbath, he cannot be a man of God. If he is a drunkard, as some say, he cannot be anything very much. If he is a crowd seducer, a lying demagogue, as others accuse him of being, his claims have no weight. Some take him for a prophet. The common people listen to him gladly, much to the frustration of both the aristocracy and the academics who dislike each other, but hate him worse. So everyone is making guesses. His claims are outrageous. They offend the establishment. They intrigue the proletariat.

This is how St. Matthew writes about it:

> When he came to the territory of Caesarea Philippi, Jesus asked his disciples, "Who do men say that the Son of Man is?" They answered, "Some say John the Baptist, others Elijah, others Jeremiah, or one of the prophets." "And you," he asked, "who do you say I am?" Simon Peter answered, "You are the Messiah, the Son of the living God."
>
> *(16:13-16)*

Note what the common people who listened to him gladly did when they assessed him. They put him at the top with their popular list of famous people who knew many of God's secrets. John the Baptist was a contemporary name, whose fame had reached them for saying sharp and uncomfortable things as he heralded the coming of a new age with a man greater than he, the laces of whose shoes John was unworthy to untie. Perhaps this was he, the latter-day Elijah, historically the prince of the prophets, the one they knew had the honored place as the immediate herald to the Messiah, the prophet for whom they always left a chair empty at the Passover in case he turned up. Or could it be Jeremiah, spoken of with such awe by the founders of the Pharisee movement? Or one of the prophets, perhaps? They cast him in the role of one who came before the *Messiah's* arrival. Yet they all, every one, had failed to make the connection.

So Jesus puts the question to his group. "Well, that's what *they* say. Now what do *you* say?"

Silence. And not uncharacteristically, Peter jumps in. Peter, the great initiator, the man with no more brains and possibly less than some of his partners in the enterprise around Jesus, but with an extraordinary if erratic courage of his convictions, and even the occasional insight.

There are times in our lives when we are surprised to hear ourselves saying what we say. I suspect that this may have been such an occasion in Peter's life. From his lips tumbles his inspired confession, "You are the Messiah." Peter has recognized Jesus for what he is. In that instant of recognition, we, all of us, are in a new ball game. For *this* ball, this rounded earth, this globe, has its God walking on it in man's clothing. Within this man's chest cavity beats the heart of God who created the world.

Note one thing. This glorious recognition did not save Peter from making more than a fool of himself several times. It did not, *at that stage,* guarantee a loyalty to the man he recognized as the Christ of God, the Messiah. There were shameful things ahead for Peter, and bitter humiliations. But the disciples are presented here and now with Peter's recognition of Jesus as the Christ. Perhaps he says what some are thinking. But he goes ahead and says it. He makes the natures of Christ, human and Divine, a spoken reality to his companions.

Discovery. Recognition. Articulation. What Peter finds himself doing and saying has something to say to the church today, to you and to me. When we meet together, not to worship but to confer, when the Diocesan Convention is held, or when representatives of the whole Episcopal Church forgather for the General Convention every three years, our self-consciousness as an institution becomes evident. Management and conservation problems preoccupy the officers of every institution; and ours, the institution of the Episcopal Church, is no exception. We debate and argue and disagree and vote and speak passionately about our housekeeping problems, sometimes at the expense of articulating why we are here in the first place: to proclaim Jesus as Christ, to make him a reality to the people who belong to us and to those who are still outside our doors. The people outside will rarely be attracted to an organization which does things well so much as by a family alive with a grasp of the reality of Christ's life. The job, as I see it, of every Christian congregation is to make a proclamation loud and clear that what we are interested in above and beyond all else is Christ Jesus: Christ crucified for New York and the world, risen for New York and the world, and to challenge the people of New York and the world to commit their lives to Jesus as Savior and Lord. We have, in other words, to be evangelistic.

I am constantly awed by people's sense of commitment to their job. Listening to me every week when I preach at St. Thomas will be lawyers I know often working sixteen hours a day. Listening to my words will be a friend, a banker, who rises at 5:00 in order to be working soon thereafter and through each day until well after the 5:30 leaving time. Listening to my words will be a youngster in his early twenties who often works until 2:00 in the morning and is back at 6:00 at the latest that same morning, day in, day out, for a prestigious publication. He loves it. He is committed to it. It is not that people are unused to commitment or unwilling to give it to their professional lives. It is that people, men and women, are strangers to spiritual commitment. It is that, in our case as the Episcopal Church (with a capital "C"), we have not yet tapped that source of energy which only commitment can bring with it. Why not? Commitment, not the mind-washed approach of the fanatic, deaf to reason, blind to the need for accommodation, impervious to consideration. I am not referring to the religiously obsessed who refuse to change their minds and never change the subject. No. Commitment. That is what Christianity is about. And where there is commitment *there is fire*. Commitment produces a force, a life force, in which the powers of the will and intellect and physical capacities are engaged because the soul is intrigued, liberated because it is enslaved gladly and without guilt, generously and without counting. All the juices are flowing, all the blood is racing, because the soul is enjoying a love experience. Not obsessed. Still less, besotted. Released into love, with all the marvelous characteristics that the love experience brings to the surface of a life.

Harness this power of commitment to the machinery of the church and its force for good would not only be noticeable but unstoppable. At present, as I see it, the church is in cultural captivity to the world. Bishops like John Spong of Newark make the situation what it is by repeating that the church needs to learn from the world. His own proposals for a review of sexual ethics stem from his conviction that the church should reflect in her teachings the present experience of the world in these matters. As though the world has the answers! I am not sure the world is sexually wiser now than it has ever been. The miseries and the fear in store for increasing thousands as AIDS makes its evil presence visible have nothing for which to thank the world's insights. The old Christian caution toward chastity has more grounds for credibility than ever before. People are soon going to be forced to consider these unpopular cautions to a life of sexual responsibility, restraint, commitment, and chastity. This is only one area among many where the church has capitulated to culture. We could fill courses of sermons with instances of it. As a matter of fact, I think we could, and should. Think them out. Think, for instance, of the whole problem of instant gratification, and apply it to people's impatience with the caution of the church which persists in refuting that time is not necessarily of the essence, but rather eternity. Think about it!

There is work to be done by the church, and an important agenda facing every Christian congregation today: to help people beyond the doors of our churches as well as within our ranks to reestablish the eternal priorities, to proclaim Christ's reality. Proclamation rather than speculation. Perhaps we need a lighthearted slogan, if you like:

Bishop Spong
has got it wrong

when he affirms that the world's wisdom should be listened to by the church, and its message tailored to where folks might like themselves to be at the moment. I am not advocating archaism. I am not advocating a siege mentality. I am preaching that the church has things to say, both old and new, about the Christ whose life fills the world, who waits to be recognized for who he is. Those things about him often run counter to the way we assume things to be, to the way we have accepted them as being. We can be blind because we are too certain that we see. The question is still the same, for us as for Peter; for that sailor as for Bishop Spong. Would we recognize him if we saw him now, or have we closed our minds to the possibility of being surprised by joy? It takes eyes of faith, minds informed, and hearts on fire. After all, he is God as well as man, and as Peter recognized and confessed, things are not always what they seem with Christ. People still stand in desperate need of being told just that.

Let's do it, for Christ's sake.

Spoiled for Choice?

I remember well my first Sunday in Oxford as an undergraduate nearly thirty-three years ago. In those days, we would race from dinner in college on Sunday evenings to the University Church in time to hear one of the great preachers who would be invited to mount the high pulpit for an 8:15 evening service. The place would be crammed, depending on the preacher. That first evening was by tradition the opportunity of the Bishop of Oxford to start the academic year for us all. He was a winner. The place was jammed. Undergraduates everywhere. Kenneth Escott Kirk was a scholar: a moral theologian, an awesome, High Church figure—he looked medieval and he knew it—and he had a silver voice and an extraordinary flow of oratory. Moreover, he was a wit. He began that night: "The choices before you! Think of the choices which lie before you. 'Choose you this day'—and how difficult some of them are for you—to have your hair long and curly like an aesthete, or wear it short and stubby, like an athlete. . . . Choose you this day."

The people of God through history have been confronted by prophets and wise men alike with the necessity to choose. "Choose you this day whom ye will serve," shouted Joshua to the assembled tribes of Israel, the elders and the heads and the judges, gathered at Shechem, "whether the gods which your fathers served that were on the other side of the flood, or the gods of the Amorites, in whose land ye dwell: but as for me and my house, we will serve the Lord" (Josh. 24:15, KJV). The people of God were confronted by the demand for choice because the days were evil, and their integrity as a people was in danger. Here they were, an emerging nation, surrounded by nations who had no love for their God, with standards and ideals repugnant to them. On that day and in that hour there was no place, no place whatever, for the comfortable doctrine that it doesn't matter what you believe so long as you do not harm anybody. It did matter. It was a matter of life and death—death as a nation if what made them special was allowed to die. What made them special was their conviction based upon the facts of history. They had a special role to play in maintaining before an unbelieving world their belief in the one true God. Between that God and their nation was a covenant. God had kept the covenant "betwixt them made." He had rescued them, saved them from servitude—miraculously. He had convinced them of their destiny. They were his people. Anything less than that conviction meant death—death to their integrity, death to their identity. Joshua saw it, saw it clearly, and made them face the issue. They faced it, and survived. They were faced with a choice.

So the words of Scripture ring out: "Before man is life and death," and then, in words that the passing of the centuries has never faded in their force: "He hath set fire and water before thee: stretch forth thy hand unto whichsoever thou wilt" (Sir. 15:16). Fire or water to choose from. There are certain terms in the Scriptures old and new, elemental terms, which are used to describe the activity of God. They are poetic and they are paradoxical. How else can we convey in human language what God is like and what he does? We rise to paradox and poetry to attempt it. You have only to look at the Psalms to see how poetry and paradox take over where human language stumbles.

Two of the most powerful images both of what God *is* and of what God *does* are fire and water. Both are mysterious elements. Both have a mysterious life. Both have the habit of appearing unexpectedly, to surprise us with their presence. Both have an element of danger. Both assist life and death. And death can come from the absence of either, as Captain Scott of the Antarctic and Bishop Pike could attest from their graves, one frozen to death and the other lost in the desert to die of thirst in the sun.

It was in the fire that the early people of God located the Divine presence. Moses was confronted by the burning bush which was not consumed, and he knew he was in the presence of God. His people looked for the fire by night to guide them and give their destiny its physical direction—to the promised land.

But fire consumes. They saw that. And thus began the understanding that you could not play with God any more than you can play with fire, for fire and the Divine judgment on human activity worked the same way. In the living, mysterious heart of the fire was the holiness and righteousness of the living God, which sin could somehow not approach without being burned to ashes like chaff of wheat. God's judgment, God's righteous power, lay in fire. Moses saw it, and trembled. And many a generation trembled, after him, and used the term in Scripture and in sacred song so to describe it. To this day we sing Henry Scott Holland's fine hymn:

Judge eternal, throned in splendor
Lord of lords, and King of kings,
With thy living fire of judgment
Purge this land of bitter things.

And there is water, mysteriously welling up from the unknown, bringing life to land and to man in the heat of the desert sun, bringing refreshment and cleansing and renewal to creation. But it also has its element of danger. You remember the flood, the Divine judgment outpoured on a nation and a world to reduce it to obedience. At the same time, those same waters were sent to save the remnant, the final few, who loved God with their lives; and so there grew, as there had grown with the consideration of the mystery of the living fire, a tradition of belief that God's activity could be described in the symbol of water, the source of life and sustenance with a power that none could stop and from which none could escape. "Let judgment roll down as waters, and righteousness as a mighty stream" (Amos 5:24, KJV), carrying the rubbish of man's disobedience in its unhindered way.

There. "He hath set fire and water before thee." Choose. "Stretch forth thine hand unto whichsoever thou wilt." Exercise your choice. The choice is unavoidable for the children of God. And the choice is this: you cannot approach God without incurring judgment upon what you are. As he comes to you there is judgment involved in his approach. Not because he delights in condemnation; he does not. With him there is a holiness, an ineffable righteousness, which all that is less in holiness and righteousness cannot approach without being consumed, burned away, carried away. Any hope of a relationship with God has embedded in it the choice the soul must make. If I want him, if I want the Lord, then I must expose for judgment, for correction, for reproof *as a requisite to my survival,* my life with its imperfections, its impurities of substance, its alloys of motive, mixed and confused in every component of my actions. I cannot look at Christ and say, "Love me, love my dog," when my dog is my sin.

The choice, you see, is between a life with him, judgment and all, with its pain and humiliation, and life without him. Life without him is a life free from the constant smart of judgment felt, at least for a time, because who is there for us to acknowledge as the reproach to our selfishness other than the earthly victims of it? And we can hide our sight from them and be deaf to their cry, if we like. But only for a time. We can for a time avoid the choice of either the fire or the water, both of which are vehicles of the Divine judgment. Or we can stretch forth our hand, the hand of need, of self-realization, the hand of penitence, the hand of hope, the hand of longing to the fire or to the water. And we flinch as we do so for we know that doing so involves us in judgment in our nearness to the Holy Lord.

But as we flinch from fear at what may be involved in our longing for nearness to him, another aspect of the fire and water make themselves known to us, for the fire of judgment we discover is none other than the fire of the love of Christ, the fire of the Spirit of Christ. We choose. We stretch forth our hand to the fire; and the testimony of the saints and the people of God is that a flame is lit within us and the Spirit working in us blows it into a fire.

O Thou who camest from above
The fire celestial to impart,
Kindle a flame of sacred love
On the mean altar of my heart.
There let it for thy glory burn
With inextinguishable blaze,

And trembling to its source return
In humble prayer and ardent praise.

We choose. We stretch out our hand to the water—and find it is the water of life, as well as the river of judgment, spoken of by John as "the water and the spirit," for a longing for God in Christ brings its own Divine thirst for more, from the never-ending spring and fountain of the Divine life, and we live "in the Spirit."

Thus, then, the paradox of a choice that seems to be no choice, a choice *not* between safety and danger, but between the life and death of the soul, in which the Lord's judgment and the Lord's own life are inseparably joined. Take courage to make this choice, and wisdom to see the choices in our lives, when there is nothing for it but to declare our need of him and his life. So again the words of a familiar hymn:

Let the fierce fires which burn and try,
Our inmost spirits purify:
Consume the ill; purge out the shame;
O God, be with us in the flame;
A newborn people may we rise,
More pure, more true, more nobly wise?

Good News, Bad News

We have all heard the "Good News, Bad News" stories. Usually they make us laugh. But it is also a story form which our Lord uses, and with devastating effect. He talks about things that are lost and get found: a coin, a sheep, a willful son. But he also talks about possessions easily assumed to be permanent and held in perpetuity from which the owner is forever parted. This is the "Good News, Bad News" bit. You hear them in the parables told by Christ himself, and they are his warnings.

The fact is that the Bible says there is the possibility of loss; in some cases, eternal loss. This constitutes an uncomfortable doctrine to which the power of positive thinking and all the self-help religious quackery have nothing much of value to say. Finding—and losing; the Psalmist can say, "The Lord gave them their hearts' desire . . . and sent leanness withal into their souls." People get what they most want, only to find when they get it that the sweet taste of possession has suddenly gone sour; they think they find, only to discover they have lost. You and I well know how some relationships can take a nosedive: people end up by losing each other after selfishly stacking the cards to obtain each other. This experience is as true for some individuals, when two people want each other selfishly, as it can be true of a nation when through the promises of "bread and circuses" a particular candidate can capture a people's vote for a position of power and worldly prestige. Once the honeymoon is over people realize what they now have after getting what they wanted, and they are sorry. And the same can be true the other way around. I have known men long for power or for a position, and lust to get it. But once it is theirs it tastes bad. And look at the man who marries the spirit of the moment; he will wake before long to find himself a widower. He thinks he has found, but in the long term he has lost.

Listen to this: "He that loveth silver shall not be satisfied with silver; nor he that loveth abundance with increase: this is also vanity" (Eccles. 5:10). Ecclesiastes, the cynical Preacher, said that. He speaks of the sense of loss that comes to the acquisitive and the possessive. Apply this to a human relationship selfishly arranged, a nation's selfish hopes in an election, an individual's lust for power, and what happens: what they think they want is not sufficient when they get it; they experience an emptiness, a loss of satisfaction. "He that loveth silver shall not be satisfied with silver."

But it is Christ who says most about all this, and most of it is disturbing, to be sure. He talks about what you do with what you have, and the terrible wish of the heart's love; where it lies. You may be sure that if the heart cleaves to what you think you have, you will stand to lose what it is that the heart has strayed to. It was Dives, the rich man, not the poor man, who in a story Jesus tells went not to heaven but endured deprivation and final loss *and knew it*. So Jesus tells us this because he wants us to know that the heart's fullest possession is God. In a striking story about a man whose barns were so full after the harvest that he decided to pull them down and build greater ones, to live off the profits of the sale of their contents, Christ adds the chilling sentence: "That night the man was told, 'Thou fool, this night shall thy soul be required of thee.'" It was all for nothing, his heart's trust in himself and all he had, for he had forgotten the fact that he was not the possessor but the steward of the good things God had provided.

The attitude toward stewardship: Matthew records four occasions of forcible exclusion, loss of possession, and terrible frustration which all refer to what people do with what they have been given. The recurring phrase is: "there shall be weeping and gnashing of teeth." The first was about those "born to the kingdom" who will be driven out into the dark, the place of wailing and gnashing of teeth; that is, those who assume they have a place find they do not. Their bland assumptions of possession are proved to have no substance and are of no eternal significance. The second concerns the man called in at the last moment to a wedding. He assumes he may dispense with the courtesy toward his host of putting on his best suit. He is shown the door—not politely. He is thrown through that door, bound hand and foot, Christ says. The third is about the bad steward who abuses his position and assumes the prerogatives of his master in ill-treating his fellow servants junior to him in rank and throwing his weight about. He is thrown out, having lost everything he held dear. The fourth is the shiftless steward, the man who did not make it, who assumes in his cowardice that he might lose the little he has been entrusted with and refuses to exercise his stewardship and his legitimate responsibilities. He also is thrown out, to that place of weeping and gnashing of teeth.

Here are four stern reminders of the possibility of terrible loss. All does *not* come right in the end. Christ tells us so. We are responsible to God. We have to answer to God. We take a risk when we claim kinship with him, when we claim for ourselves certain prerogatives in our relationship with him. It is true that there are times—and Christ warns the church—when the last shall be judged first, *and the first last*. There are times when our assumptions about our place in the scheme of things are "weighed in the balance and found wanting," when our assessments of our worth have been pitted against someone else's, to their disadvantage, only for us to discover that what we thought we had found in ourselves was imaginary. So we stand to lose what we think we have, what we think is ours by right. This is sobering stuff, sobering enough to make us look to our laurels: sobering enough to make us realize as Christians that the Lord whom we profess to own and serve requires of us more *availability* than assumption of possession. The French have a word for it: *disponibilité,* the attitude: "Here am I Lord; send me . . ." for we may not presume as to who shall have the last possession in our lives. There is an arrogance in the words of the poet William Ernest Henley—"I am the master of my fate, I am the captain of my soul." No. For there is someone else, Some One else, who is both Master of fates and Captain of souls, who can say: "If anyone wishes to be a follower of mine, he must leave self behind; he must take up his cross and come with me. Whoever cares for his own safety is lost; but if a man will let himself be lost *for my sake,* he will find his true self. *What will a man gain* by winning the whole world, at the cost of his true self?" (Matt. 16:24-26).

There is the rub. But there is the clue, also. The good news is right there among the bad news. To a world and a generation concerned with self-discovery, self-finding, self-aggrandizement, self-assurance, feeling good about oneself, and all the activities we can engage in so that we are better able to relate, to communicate, to succeed, to become a millionaire in a matter of months, to be sexually compatible with all comers, to have a deeper voice, to stand an inch taller, to grow hair on bald spots, to make friends and influence people, all the self-achievement upon which we set so much store—to this world and generation the Christ of Galilee and of our day has a warning. He tells us in no uncertain terms that that way, all can be lost; all, that is, of eternal significance, and furthermore that it is eternity in the end that matters. Our true self-discovery is in losing ourselves in love for him, in glad obedience to him, and in him ultimately to the Father. Our destiny is in him. Our winning is in our reliance upon his sacrifice, his redemption of us through his cross. Our treasure troves are his promises for us and for the world he has made and redeemed with his most precious blood. Our home, our barns, our store, our hopes for fresh beginnings in our lives with others lie with our first beginnings with him: our penitence, our self-naughting, our self-forgetfulness in his sight.

For *his* work is plain: "I have come down from heaven, not to do my own will, but the will of him who sent me. It is his will that *I should not lose even one* of all that he has given me, but raise them all up on the last day" (John 6:38-39).

That means you. And me. That is why he warns us so sternly, for it is eternity that matters.

One man learned that lesson keenly. He loved life. He loved to express himself in the love of his God. I suppose if he had lived in our day he might have written for *Playboy,* whose "lust is for life"; his poetry is hot enough. But he learned. He learned because he lost much and stood to lose more, with all he thought he had. John Donne recognized Christ's stern warning and cried out:

I shall not live till I see God
And when I have seen him, I shall
never die.

How on Earth Do I Believe in Heaven?

ALL of us have the capacity to believe what we want to believe. We do it with people we know and we do it with people we do not know. Popular publications help this process. Look at *Enquirer* or *People* to read what the Princess of Wales is alleged to have done or to have said. People build up fantasies about the famous; they leap to the pages of these magazines and devour the stories they contain (in order to sell them), believing what they want to believe. An unadorned presentation of accurate facts leaves them cold. They want to believe the unusual, the improbable, the impossible. A new play here in New York, *A Pack of Lies,* is about two families, neighbors and friends for decades. Together they are caught up in an agony when the house of one family is used by the police to survey the comings and goings of the other, suspected of spying for Russia. The family whose house is used is outraged by the imputation of treason on the part of their friends. The wife simply will not consider believing the suspicion, as beneath her integrity and contrary to her loyalties. It makes an interesting situation for a play. But it is not a fairy tale. There was such a case. And the people were adamant in their initial refusal to believe. Coming to terms with reality was excruciating.

Some people simply cannot do so. When their dream world is shattered, they are shattered. Reality can be too much for them. T. S. Eliot was right: "Mankind cannot bear very much reality."

In his encounter with Nicodemus, our Lord makes use of a formula which requires people to listen and respond. Nicodemus is a Jewish leader, a Pharisee, a member of the Sanhedrin Council of Seventy, and famous as a teacher in Israel. He has taken the initiative to seek Jesus out for a conversation about important matters. Jesus is adamant: "unless a man has been born over again he cannot see the kingdom of God." Nicodemus has trouble with the concept and says so. Jesus expresses his disappointment with him: "What! . . . Is this famous teacher of Israel ignorant of such things? In very truth I tell you, we speak of what we know, and testify to what we have seen, and yet you all reject our testimony. If you disbelieve me when I talk to you about things on earth, how are you to believe if I should talk about the things of heaven?" (John 3:10-12). Christ tackles the mind-set of Nicodemus and others head-on. In the face of his testimony, based on knowledge and sight, there is rejection: "Don't confuse us with the facts." It is not a question of withholding assent to belief because of doubts; it is a question of *refusing* to consider assent because of certainties. We all know how ugly bigotry can be: a mind closed to any other consideration apart from its preoccupation. Ears deaf to reason, to logic, to persuasion; eyes blinkered to the narrow vision already chosen: religious bigotry, political bigotry, ethnic bigotry—all are vile, and all reduce the cause espoused as well as the cause disavowed. All also reduce the soul of the bigot.

Christ knows this will happen. He knows that a soul can be deformed, stunted, by its refusal to exercise the muscles of its faith. My grandfather, when we were children, would tease us when we complained of an ache or pain without good reason: "I can see that amputation is setting in." "Amputation sets in," if you like, when the soul balks at exercising the muscles of its faith, so that it becomes unable to tackle the larger issues and hear the fine music because of its preoccupation with its perception of the truth.

In truth, people can be too certain about things. They talk as if they know. The fact is, we do not know as much as we think we know. Who says so? Christ says so. "No one knows the Son but the Father, and no one knows the Father but the Son and those to whom the Son may choose to reveal him" (Matt. 11:27). Yet the people of God have little heeded this warning. Far too often they have refused to take it seriously, in their assumption that they are the sole repository for the Divine revelation.

I want, if possible, to be a dissuader of fundamentalism. "But now I am cabin'd, cribb'd, confin'd, bound in to saucy doubts and fears"—this could well be a description of the soul which cannot tolerate any doctrine that differs from what it personally has perceived as the truth. Behind the wish for authoritarianism is fear. Whether "the Bible says" or "Holy Mother Church says," fear and ignorance combined, and under any banner, even that of the Cross of Christ, is an ugly phenomenon. It is ugly because it is a caricature, a misbegotten infant of the mind. There was a time when the Latin tag *Extra ecclesiam nulla salus est* ("Outside the church there is no salvation") was repeated in order to reassure the members within it that their safety was certified. Nowadays that statement, though it has elements of the truth, is no longer bandied about. It has been manifestly proven shallow, judgmental, and lacking in the Divine generosity. The reason for repeating it at all is fear and ignorance. The *cause* for it is the fatal human habit of fencing God into the mirror reflection of our own personalities. Sir George Grenfell Baines once described it to me as "making God in our own image." You are aware that some people relish sermons on the Divine wrath and vengeance in treating the theme of the Last Judgment. Might it not possibly be a projection of their own vindictiveness, their own desire for revenge? Amos Starkadder's sermon in *Cold Comfort Farm,* meant to scare the living daylights out of its rustic hearers, carries this view to its ridiculous conclusion. Amos was an old scoundrel and we discern it in the story. We have a capacity for *exclusion:* we relish that part of the "I'm OK; You're OK" process that says I'm OK; you're not OK.

But this attitude Christ steadfastly combats. There is the question of truth. The apprehension of that same truth may take differing paths, and emphases may differ in the proclamation of it. One of the reasons I am a Christian of the Anglican persuasion is that our church is prepared, often at its own cost, to uphold this truth. It is derided as being theologically untidy. It is criticized for being timid in its theological statements. It is dismissed as wishy-washy, evasive of precision and careless about its contradictions. I maintain it is generous. It makes adult demands and expects adult responses from its members. It does not claim to know all the answers. It acknowledges wisdom and insight into the things of the Spirit from sources which are neither favorable of it nor respectful to it. It resists the temper of the persecutor after repenting for its own bloodstained history of persecuting Christians of other persuasions. The Roman Catholics had a hard time of it in the sixteenth and seventeenth and eighteenth centuries. Protestants were discriminated against and our loss was the secession from us of Christians sneeringly referred to as Methodists. We have penitently come to learn through its many mistakes and its corporate sins of narrowness, discrimination, and proprietary attitudes toward buildings, properties, and people's lives that there is a more excellent way. And Paul, of all people, who is demanding, exacting, theologically passionate for purity of the understanding of the person and work of Christ, could say this:

> I have made myself every man's servant, to win over as many as possible. To Jews I became like a Jew, to win Jews; as they are subject to the Law of Moses, I put myself under that law to win them, although I am not myself subject to it. To win Gentiles, who are outside the Law, I made myself like one of them, although I am not in truth outside God's law, being under the law of Christ. To the weak I became weak, to win the weak. Indeed I have become everything in turn to men of every sort, so that in one way or another I may save some. All this I do for the sake of the Gospel.
>
> *(1 Cor. 9:19-23)*

In other words, there is no Christian justification for insisting that truth about God can be perceived only in the narrow reaches of one's own personal grasp of it. Beware of equating truth with precision. "There's a wideness in God's mercy like the wideness of the sea. . . . For the love of God is broader than the measure of man's mind" (Faber). And the proclamation of that mercy and that love can be seen to be true in startling fullness in the lips and lives of those who do not interpret the truths of them in the way we have received them and perceived them. No one Christian body has the exclusive monopoly of the Divine truth, just as no one Christian body has exclusive claim to the interpretation of the Word of God in Scripture. We must remember that, and remember it steadfastly as we make the claim for the truth of the fact that Jesus is Lord of Christ's Holy Catholic Church of which we are a part, living its life in Order and Sacrament. Rather than reject, our duty is to respect. Rather than forbid, our duty is in Paul's words to "prove that which is good," which means to welcome and to encourage insights into the workings of God in Christ known by their fruits, and as Paul tells us in his letter to the Galatians, the fruits of that Spirit of Christ are "Love, joy, peace, patience, kindness, goodness, fidelity, gentleness, and self-control" (Gal. 5:22). These leave little room for the contentious spirit of comparison or exclusion, of cloaking our own ignorances and anxieties under a clever camouflage of spiritual concern for purity of doctrine. Eschew a religion which discourages you from the obligation to *think,* and think hard.

For the majestic point about Christ's warning and injunction is that there is no yawning divide between things of earth and the things of heaven about which he wants to tell us; they are all of God. Christ in himself has joined the things of earth and the things of heaven into a single peace, and what he says is all about himself, and his role as God incarnate, Emmanuel, God living with us. He offers not so much assured answers about himself as assured *access* to himself if we would be born again, with honesty of approach and humility of those who are unafraid, for "No one ever went up into heaven except the one who came down from heaven, the Son of Man whose home is in heaven."

Meeting People Halfway

THERE is one phrase in our language which for its insensitivity and arrogance is calculated to be among the world's top ten turn-offs: "I can read you like a book." We may have a shrewd idea of what goes on in the mind of a friend or lover; we may think alike and we may prefer the same things. We may share the same hopes for our children, our homes, our lives. And we may exhibit the same instinctive reactions to things. Nevertheless, however deep our knowledge goes into the character of a human being beside ourselves, however cleverly we calculate a response, given all sorts of data from previous responses in previous situations, there must always be left a space for the unexpected. Carefully handled, this makes for the stuff of humor, and *very* carefully handled it can even become hilarious. The great actress, Beatrice Lilley, made this her strongest and funniest weapon. To see her as the curtains went up, looking regal and lovely and singing most marvelously an aria, singing it straight and singing it strong—and then, hitching up her long skirts and rollerskating off the stage into the wings, is a case in point. You could never read Beatrice Lilley like a book, however well you knew her repertoire.

The fact remains that there *are* people whose predictability is a byword, whose reactions to situations are almost universally known. And of course there are like-minded groups, political and ethnic and religious, whose "readability" is dangerously tempting. Among such, and preeminent, were the Pharisees. They were famous or infamous, whichever way you looked at it, for their uncompromising observance of the Law of Moses as it was interpreted by their rabbis. They could be relied upon to uphold the most insignificant point of the law. It was their vocation as Pharisees, as "separated ones," to do just that. It was their vocation, their mission, the lodestar of their life, to maintain the religious purity of the Jewish nation. And in order to do so they separated themselves from the hoi polloi, the careless observers and the lukewarm believers, those tinged with heretical beliefs and practices of the pagan and Greek civilizations which surrounded them. They were the hard core of resisters to foreign infiltration of the Jewish faith. They made no room for compromise with Greek ideas and ideals, such as did the Sadducees, the Jewish aristocracy, whose sons wore Greek hats and joined in the shocking practice of nudity at the gymnasium. One such High Priest even took a Greek name, Jason. But not the Pharisees. They were holy terrors: holy and terrors.

But what about a *Pharisee of the Pharisees? The* Pharisee of the Pharisees, self-confessed? Saul of Tarsus, Paul as he became, was to claim his ancestral angularity and awkwardness as Pharisee of the Pharisees with pride. Not seemingly much space there for compromise in his makeup or his track record of intellectual toughness or suffering later gladly borne for the sake of his Lord. When he in his own words put off the old man and put on Christ, when he took to himself the yoke and cloak of Christ, when he gave himself to his Lord on the Damascus Road, we are not told that he shed his Pharisaism. He carried it with him, transfigured but still there. He did not cease to be the Jew from Tarsus, and he still acknowledged his education in the law under Gamaliel. Yet he was no longer wholly predictable, readable, for in the first letter he wrote to the Corinthians he said, "For my part I always try to meet everyone half-way, regarding not my own good but the good of the many, so that they may be saved" (1 Cor. 10:33).

I suggest that this innocent, easy little phrase is one of the most significant remarks Paul ever could let drop about the nature of his faith's change, his conversion to Christ. For he now lives and operates in a dimension totally new and immeasurably grander than that of his birth. He has made a great discovery and here is an indication of it: that in Christ—and in the following breath he alludes to it—he has the example and authority for saying that for his part he always tries to meet everyone halfway, not for his own good but for the good of many, so that they may be saved.

He has, in other words, hit upon a keener, deeper understanding of an area in the lives of people around him, seen in the light of Christ, that blinding light of the Damascus Road, and deep in the heart of the mystery of Divine forgiveness. Whereas compromise in his old life was a sign of weakness and worldliness, now in his new life it is something else. Christian compromise comes from Christ's strength. It has a potential for good; it can assist in the salvation of souls. Christian compromise is different just because in Christ everything is different, because it is new, it is the fruit of his re-creation. He is the fulfillment of the law he came not to destroy but to fulfill. That old law which so tightly bound Saul the Pharisee is seen anew by Paul the Pharisee Apostle. The more he hears of what Christ said and taught, the more aware he becomes of the new freedom which stems from the Divine pardon and forgiveness.

What does Christ say? And to whom does he say it? To the Pharisees, usually. "Render unto Caesar the things that are Caesar's, and to God the things that are God's." These are legitimate claims which an alien state, a pagan state, can make upon a citizen. There is no need to pretend that by disagreeing with the lack of religious integrity of the state we are absolved from our citizenship's responsibilities, our legal commitments to a legal demand. Here is a profound compromise, a deep issue, which has through the centuries caused much heart searching. It points to the truth that we cannot opt out of this world because we do not approve of what goes on in it. It points to the mystery that the honor we pay to God is in the setting of this present world with all its blemishes, its fallenness. It points to the truth that in perfectionism there is pride, that in judging we are usurping the Divine prerogative. We have to come to Christ's terms with the world, go halfway, not reject it or pretend it is not there, for God made it, and in it and in the institutions which sinful men establish, his glory and his service are to be found and offered. There *is* a compromise and we do well to observe it. It is a delicate compromise which has been mishandled many times. The church has leaned too hard one way and then the other. Holy men have made a mistaken withdrawal from their responsibilities to the world's needs and demands—and it was to men who had opted out of their responsibilities to work and provide for their families because they were convinced that Christ's second coming was immediately imminent that Paul himself could declare in irritation, "If a man will not work, neither let him eat"—that is, if he will not face his worldly responsibilities and go halfway, he deserves to be reminded vigorously.

Or, Christ says, "Be careful not to make a show of your religion before men; if you do, no reward awaits you in your Father's house in heaven" (Matt. 6:1). If anything could cut at the rigorist line to men of his time and since, this warning does. By ensuring that some people *were* made aware of the religion one professed, by wearing the phylactery or headband with sentences of the Law of Moses written into it, or by abstaining from food considered unclean, or eating it with unwashed hands, one spurned the compromise with the unbelieving world. But Christ tells us the opposite, for he says that his Father sees what is done in secret: in the depths and ground of the heart. And *that* is important to the Father who made and makes and loves all people, Greek or Jew, bond or free, male or female. Christ's compromise erodes proud judgments, tears self-consciousness to tatters, lifts the service of God from the notion of notching my spiritual sword with victories I have won in the struggle with uncaring humanity. We are to go halfway; to stand and be counted for him—yet not so as to alienate and cause scandal to souls who, however less well they worship, may still please the Father who sees in secret. It is delicate, it is damnably difficult. But that is what he wants, and we must see that he gets it.

Or again he says, "Pass no judgment, and you will not be judged." Why then were we given our critical faculties? When then are we expected to uphold standards and maintain principles? What are morals for? I ask these questions of a Christ who refuses to allow me to judge, having given me all these things in my heritage as a Christian. "No," he says firmly to me, "you are in no position to judge. You may look around you as you work and as you worship and see people whose social and sexual standards and predilections are not necessarily those you have for yourself. Their presence may disturb you; their lives may not commend themselves to you and the way you live. If you judge because you are threatened, you do wrong. If you judge because you dislike them and their way, you are wrong. You have to go halfway to them," he says to me. "I love them as I love you. I died for them as I died for you. I am the judge, and my judgment is unlike your judgment. My judgment is another aspect of my love and mercy; yours is not. *Your* job is to extend my mercy. And how can you extend it if you do not go halfway?"

I have given three examples from many. All can convict us with their force, as Paul the Pharisee of the Pharisees was aware when he wrote his claim. This Christian compromise based upon the mercy of Christ, the tenderness of Christ, the mystery of Christ's life among us, is part of the church's delicate task of presenting him to the world; for we who are in the church are in Paul's words "messengers of reconciliation." And how can we offer the reconciliation we bring—*his* love, *his* forgiveness, *his* acceptance—if our arms are not stretched out like his to greet and to welcome and to console? The Lord in the deathless story of the prodigal son precisely says what the father did when his months of waiting were over and his boy appeared in sight: "But while he was still a long way off his father saw him, and his heart went out to him. He *ran to meet him, flung his arms round him, and kissed him*" (Luke 15:20). That halfway meeting made all the difference between heaven and hell.

Facing Up to It

YOU never know what you will see next in New York. One Sunday afternoon last summer in Central Park, a crowd was looking at something. There on a bench stood a lovely great dog, a whitish German Shepherd, painted by his master with black stripes like a zebra. Why he had been painted like that is a typical New York mystery.

A typical Galilee mystery was the habit Christ had of saying traffic-stopping things to his disciples. They, like New Yorkers, never knew what next to expect from him. The more I read what he says, the more often I stop to think what he is saying, the more astounding it is that he says the things he says. I am convinced that he says what he says because he is what he is. But he says things the world has never heard before, things it has never thought before, even for a second, and the things he says are sometimes claims he makes. These claims are stupendous. They take one's breath away for their boldness. They are an affront to the world's experience, to its wisdom, to its capacity for belief.

Get this straight. His claims are either a matter of life or death for us if they are true or, if they are not true, not only is the whole construction of our faith as vulnerable as a house of cards but the person around whom it is constructed is a diseased perpetrator of cruel fables, a liar, a cheat, a swindler of people's affections and the thief of the hope of the poor.

One such claim was that "I am in the Father and the Father in me." Listen to what occasions this extraordinary remark to his disciples. St. John records it in his Gospel, chapter 14, verses 1-10.

From the mouth of the stolid and embarrassingly obtuse patron saint of my church on Fifth Avenue, Thomas the Doubter, comes the question, "How can we know the way?" and Jesus' answer, "I am the way. . . . No one comes to the Father except by me. If you knew me you would know my Father too" (vv. 6-7). This leads to Philip's request, which, to a group of people whose firm belief it was as Jews that not only was God invisible but that he was unseeable, is preposterous: "Lord, show us the Father, and we shall be satisfied" (v. 8). That was a piece of cheek for a start. It was not merely totally out of line for a Jewish man to request, but to suggest it at all shows a crass misunderstanding of what Jesus has been saying about the relationship he and the Father share.

"Lord, show us the Father, and we shall be satisfied." But every man there knew that even to Moses, who was vouchsafed a glimpse of that glory, God had said that he would not show his face. Moses would have to be satisfied, as the Scriptures describe it, with God's "back." Whatever that means, we can know that there was no display to Moses of the full vision of God. And here is Philip asking for just that. And the answer? You want to see God? Take a look at me.

Look at Jesus and you will see what God is like. You will see several things. I will list six.

1. *You look into the face of a humble God.* That is possibly the most devastating discovery you can make about God. The decision to intervene personally in our history by appearing without fanfare and without trappings of celestial majesty but rather as one of the displaced poor states a preferential option on the part of the Divine Creator: he aligns himself to those who have very little, who have few hopes of anything much more, to those who are not thought of in terms of influence or accomplishment or even a place in the sun. God is seen in the forgotten, in the forgettable, with all the nuisance value that the needy have for us, at our elbow, looking at us, expecting, quite rightly, that because we are in a position to help, we will help. It may help you to be humble by being on guard against the constant thrust and push of the self over others, but nothing will help you more to be humble than by looking into the face of a humble God.

2. *You look into the face of a God who knows exhaustion.* The constant search for souls, the never-ending proclamation of uncomfortable truth, the never-ending self-giving, the ceaseless bringing of healing of soul and body, the whole effort, in fact, of *life-giving*, of restoration, reclamation, renewal, redemption, without thought for the satisfaction of his own human needs, for rest, for affirmation, for hospitality, so that in the end, after saying that the Son of Man "hath no place to lay his head," he dies without the possession of a tomb to put his body in, are instances of this. Who is it who says, "My Father works, and I work," and the word he uses is for hard, unrelenting slog, physically exhausting labor? It is God whom we look at in the face of Christ. But his determination to offer all his resources for our benefit, our betterment, our blessedness, shows us how costly it is to be God. Remember that work, labor, is the ancient curse of fallen humanity. God's terrible words to Adam in the Garden of Eden after the disobedience—"By the sweat of your face you shall eat bread" (Gen. 3:19)—are taken willingly to himself. He bears a curse and takes it to himself. I think this is a terrible and dark mystery. God sweats for us.

3. *You look into the face of a God who knows temptation.* "Tempted in all things, as we are" is a description of Christ and God who knows not merely the itch and pull of temptation but the physical and spiritual agony of never giving in. Sensitive to it, wracked by it, always aware of it, and never succumbing to it. The idea of God being above what makes monkeys of us is simply absurd. The keenness of it cuts him more painfully than it cuts us, who are used to capitulation and the temporary easing of the strain.

4. *You look into the face of a giving God.* From our earliest days, we cling to what we have. A baby finger will grasp, not to let go. We amass our possessions. They are our defenses: from our friendships to our habits; from our plans for our lives to our prejudices; from what we inherit to what we earn however lawfully. We acquire. We build. We invest. And we spend a lot of time in this activity. God's personality, if you think about it for a moment, is entirely other. He gives himself to us in his church and his life in the Sacraments. He imparts joy. He begets hope. He is the source of strength, all our strengths. He is the fountain of logic, of truth, of

farsightedness and wisdom. The friends he gathers are not to bolster a needy ego. He gathers them because in him they can be friends with each other, help each other, serve each other, sacrifice for each other. All he does is give himself away to the world and embrace it in the arms of his steady love.

5. *You look into the face of a God who knows anger.* But not the anger of which we are capable: personal anger that can strike to wound. Divine anger, rather, is utterly bereft of personal displeasure. It is a distancing from evil, not by withdrawing from it but by approaching it so that it is singed and burned by the pure fire of the Divine love. Evil cannot take that fire. You see it in those who fled from the avenging scourge in Christ's hand when he cleansed the Temple. Christ's anger cleanses. If you cannot face that, do not get near him. And at this point I ought to remind you and myself that when people complain that God somehow is absent or distant from them and their prayers, and resent it, there is one question: Who moved?

6. *You look into the face of a victorious God.* Not a successful God. A victorious God. A God with scars. With wounds. Suffering has marred his face more than any man's, disfigured it with pain and loneliness. It is the face of a God who knows what hurt is, what devastation and depletion are, what it means to lose your dignity and what it means to be shut out and excluded, how cold contempt can feel, and how hot hatred can scald. But it is the face of a God who has stared at all this, all the evil in the world. He has engaged it, wrestled with it and has seemed to lose, only to show that love has a life stronger and livelier than the deadening of death. He has come up again from the earth, literally, the man from down under. For, let's finally face it, in Archbishop Michael Ramsey's marvelous phrase: "God is Christlike and in him is no un-Christlikeness at all."

Can Any Good Thing Come out of Canarsie?

EVERYONE must have seen the famous poster of New York that appeared years ago on the cover of the *New Yorker.* Manhattan stands in the foreground. The rest of America and the rest of the world are seen as little lumps on a sparse landscape.

There is a scriptural warrant for it. The world of New York and the world of first-century Palestine have much in common. Listen: "Philip went to find Nathanael, and told him, 'We have met the man spoken of by Moses in the Law, and by the prophets: it is Jesus son of Joseph, from Nazareth.' 'Nazareth!' Nathanael exclaimed; 'Can anything good come from Nazareth?'" (John 1:45-46).

Nathanael came from Cana. Big deal. What was worse, the wedding had not yet happened, to give the place its rightful fame. It was a scrubby town, with all the grubby rivalry and prejudice of a small town. Remember the poster. Forget Manhattan's hassle, the noise, the frustration, the subway horrors, the expense, the street surfaces, and thumb your nose to Hackensack, Elizabeth, and Hoboken, or whatever strikes your fancy to ridicule and scorn just because you are *here*. And if you're here, if only by your fingertips, you have arrived. Can any good thing come out of Canarsie?

Think again about what I quoted. Listen again. It is a declaration of a spiritual discovery. It is a testimony if you like, in the old evangelical sense: "'*We have met* the man spoken of by Moses in the Law, and by the prophets: it is Jesus son of Joseph from Nazareth.' 'Nazareth! . . . Can any good thing come from Nazareth?'"

A man proclaims a personal encounter with the Messiah who fulfills all the law and all prophecy. It is a declaration of faith. And this is what the churches say: "We have met . . . Jesus of Nazareth." And now as on the day that first declaration was made that same proclamation is doubted because its origins are dubious.

This is the story of the church in disunity and disarray. It is the indictment of the Christian world, that one set of its people should take leave to doubt the spiritual authenticity of another, and to say so in those precise and wounding terms, can anything good come from *there*?

For many years now, through this century, the church has nevertheless thought to put aside this one week each year, from January 18 to 25, to mourn our divisions, to repent our prejudices, to seek new humility toward those who proclaim they have met Jesus of Nazareth in a different way and from a different approach, and to see how best we can, by coming closer to him, come closer to each other.

That has not been easy. Certain prerequisites have been ignored, of which I will mention a few later. These prerequisites are a *sine qua non*—without which nothing can happen. And so the state of things is that nothing of significance can really at present be expected to happen.

Sad as I am to say it, I fear the cause of Christian unity has been damaged more through *overcertainty* than through neglect. There has been too much confident talking-up, on all sides and from every angle. Schemes have been concocted, plans have been laid, dates have been set, concordats have been drafted, and all too *in*frequently has any further unity between Christians been achieved. I have watched Anglican-Methodist approaches and schemes fail twice in England. The "unity by 1970 (or 1980)" plans between Protestant churches and the Anglican Church have simply not materialized. The impetus in the moves between Anglicans and Roman Catholics begun in March 1966 which Archbishop Michael Ramsey's visit to Pope Paul VI inaugurated has flagged and ecumenism limps along—many Anglicans thinking that the Polish Pope is provincial (Can any good thing come out of Poland?) and obdurate, many Romans deploring the advent of women into the priesthood of the Anglican Church, and the theological untidiness which permits some Anglicans flatly to deny what some other Anglicans declare as theological support for their position.

With the Orthodox churches of the East—Greece, Russia, Rumania, Serbia, Armenia, and Africa—the steps toward unity have often taken the pattern "one forward, two back." There seems to be an open lack of interest in pursuing unity, at least unity such as we know it, because Orthodox conceptions of unity are perhaps light-worlds away from ours. Theirs are based on the cohesion, the total pattern holding together, of their doctrine, like an icon with every detail correctly in place. Disturb one tiny detail of doctrine and you ruin the icon or picture of the concept of unity. Christians who are not in the Orthodox churches seldom have their beliefs tied up so neatly. The Orthodox churches say that unless you do, there is not much use in discussion. Can any good thing come from the Book of Common Prayer or from the history of the Episcopal Church?

Our views of unity are distinctly less defined. We are less interested in uniformity. All you have to do is to take one look to see that Episcopalians do not possess theological tidiness within our structure. The variations you can discern are alarmingly obvious. Try God in New York City. Go into St. Bartholomew's. Go into St. Mary the Virgin. Compare and contrast how God is worshiped and what is preached. Emphases differ. Details vary. Compared with some churches in the diocese we at St. Thomas must appear as though we belong to another planet, if not to another age. Can any good thing come out of St. Thomas? Can any good thing come out of St. Bart's? *We* teach through precision in worship, through biblically-based sermons and careful exposition of the Word of God, through the best music of which we are capable given the unique privilege we enjoy of a choir school and a superb set of musicians. No way can the cracks which make us stand out as different from one another in theological emphases and liturgical priorities be papered over.

Try God in the Episcopal Church of this whole country. There is continuing resentment and opposition in many hearts to the idea of women being allowed priesthood, even though there are now nearly six hundred of them, many pursuing dedicated ministries in all sorts of taxing and difficult situations. Some indeed misuse their sacred trust by harnessing their priesthood to political and feminist alliances. Their male opponents sometimes abuse their sacred trust by cloaking their misogyny with spirituality and harnessing *their* priesthood to prejudices unworthy of Christian men. We see organizations set up against the Book of Common Prayer voted by the General Convention in 1979 to be used in the churches, and we see bishops and clergy alike riding roughshod over those who find difficulty with it. Everywhere we look, there are differences, dissension, dissatisfaction, and defeatism, with what people either think the church is not preaching and practicing vigorously enough, or with what they see to be the liberties with truth and with tradition which the church is taking.

The Bishop of New York would state the prime mission of the church in one way. It is almost to be counted upon that I would state it in another. And we both think of ourselves as liberal Catholics of the Anglican persuasion. Can any good thing come out of diocesan headquarters? Can any good thing come from One West Fifty-third Street?

But take a look at the Roman Catholic Church. It was at one time monolithic in its approach to faith and morals. *Roma locuta est: res finita est.* Rome has spoken: the matter is over with. Support for women to be admitted to priesthood is sustained and in some places strident. The women of the church in America are by no means in unanimous agreement with its teachings on contraception or abortion. Its men by no means settle submissively under what it says about divorce. Its liturgies are derided by the faithful and its worship found wanting. Its bishops' statements on the nuclear defense schemes are opposed by some. Can any good thing come from the National Conference of Bishops? Can any good thing come from the conservative Vatican? Perhaps the man in this country who in himself typifies these differences and therefore draws most controversy to himself is the new Archbishop of New York, who seems to have few friends, no matter where you look. Can any good thing come from Scranton to the Archbishop's residence? Is nothing that he says of any authenticity? Can any good thing come from those who think he is misguided? His approaches inflammatory? His taste questionable?

All I am attempting to show here is the temper of our times: our unwillingness to impart integrity to approaches different from our own—our history, our experience, our spiritual grasp, our liturgical taste. It is a dangerous temper. It is a temper which will end in defeat. "Judge not that ye be not judged," says our Lord in a stern commandment which is forever being brushed under the carpet of our primrose path, wide and well paved, to our spiritual dereliction.

For again and again, we have tried through words to encapsulate the Lord in a package acceptable to us as well as understandable to us, and the disunity among the churches is the sad result. Men have fought and died about the form the Blessed Trinity has taken; have cursed each other, condemned each other to hell, split nations, ruined families, refused baptism, and denied the sacramental food and access to healing and forgiveness for those who failed to agree. Theologians have wrangled and written polemics about the presence of Christ in the Eucharist, as though anybody could ever say for sure, and the wreckage of Reformation hatreds lies around us still in prejudice and the pride of argument and words.

We ought to be thoroughly ashamed of ourselves. And we are not. We are right in respecting the need for intellectual struggle to discover more about God, but we are meant to grow in the love as well as in the knowledge of the God whom no man hath seen at any time. For he who says he loves God and hates his brother, how can the truth be in him?

I am not pleading for an anti-intellectualist approach toward the mystery of the faith we all proclaim so poorly and practice so paralytically. I am pleading for an attitude which respects new suggestions and new insights which may be jarring, may trouble us and even frighten us, as we "hold fast to that which is good," as St. Paul says, of the "faith once and for all delivered to the saints." I am pleading for an attitude which respects the church's task as the Body of Christ to teach sound doctrine, which respects what orthodoxy can mean and not what we necessarily want that word to mean. The Sunday within the Octave of Prayer for Christian Unity ought to be our observation of the most searing penitence and sorrow for messing about with a loving, courteous, hidden Christ in whom the whole Godhead dwells, from whose sacred heart both love and sorrow flow at our detestable cocksureness and tawdry triumphalism. We ought to be thoroughly ashamed and humbly ask God's love to flow through our hearts of brick, for we shall never come anywhere near to the unity he so wants to give until his holiness "becomes our inner clothing," as Christ prayed for us to enjoy, until we catch a true glimpse of that wondrous face, so that when we shall awake after his likeness, we shall be satisfied with it; and be delighted that others also share it.

Too Fat to Get through That Door

ONCE upon a time, there lived a mayor of a city in the north of England. He was one of the town's success stories. He had started small. He had worked hard. He had made his money. He sought political office, and unlike many we frequently hear of in the press, his attempt at political involvement was successful. He put the mayor's gold chain around his neck. He appeared in the newspapers often. He was a success story in himself. He rested, as they say, on his laurels. He grew fat on it, literally as well as metaphorically. He was a churchgoer. He also disliked the rector of the town who was my employer and far too honest a man to pretend that things were going well if they were not. There was a scene one day. I knew it was coming—I half hoped I would be around to see it. Whatever it was that the mayor said I am not quite clear. But whatever he said maddened the parish priest who addressed him like this: "Mr. Mayor, you're complacent. Remember, it was complacency that broke our Lord's heart."

Not ingratitude. Not impurity. Not ineffectiveness. Not dishonesty. Complacency. Do you wonder why he said that? I think I know. My old boss knew his Scriptures. If you know your Scriptures, you will easily recall one of the most frightening and frightful things Christ is ever recorded as saying. St. Luke records it. This piece of Scripture possibly holds the clue, for it is supremely recorded against complacency. Listen:

> Struggle to get through the narrow door; for I tell you that

many will try to enter and will not be able.

When once the master of the house has got up and locked the door, you may stand outside and knock, and say, "Sir, let us in!", but he will only answer, "I do not know where you come from." Then you will begin to say, "We sat at table with you and you taught in our streets." But he will repeat, "I tell you, I do not know where you come from. Out of my sight, all of you, you and your wicked ways!" There will be wailing and grinding of teeth there, when you see Abraham, Isaac, and Jacob, and all the prophets, in the kingdom of God, and yourselves thrown out. From east and west people will come, from north and south, for the feast in the kingdom of God. Yes, and some who are now last will go first, and some who are first will be last.

(Luke 13:24-30)

There is enough in that to scare the living daylights out of all of us. It is deeply disturbing, for it raises several uncomfortable issues, unavoidable issues, which none of us individually can hope to defer, postpone, or deflect.

The first is the *struggle.* Christ says flatly in answer to the question, "Are only a few to be saved?" that the door is narrow and to get through it there is a struggle, and the word he uses is a word we use: agony. Agonize—there is a measure of suffering in the determination to negotiate that narrow door. What makes it too narrow for the many who try and, as Christ says, somehow cannot get through it? Frankly, they are too fat. Fat with what they think are their deserts; fat with their assumptions of ability, their suitability for inclusion. Their expectations are large. They are based upon fleeting acquaintances with Christ. "We sat at table with you and you taught in our streets." The assumption is that Christ has been seen and noticed in *their* world: at parties of *their* friends; walking and talking in the places with which they are familiar; on property they own: "our streets." But you cannot treat Christ our Lord and God as a sort of outsider allowed in to mix with your friends and on your property. "The earth is the Lord's, and all that therein is; the compass of the world and all that dwell therein." The Psalmist of old said that.

There is an assumption here that God is somehow on the outside looking in on a world we own and whose destiny we somehow control, or in which we are at least shareholders. We delude ourselves with thinking that we are the center of the universe and everything which happens does so somehow in reaction to that fact. We make assumptions which deprive us of entry through that narrow door. The Psalmist, as usual, has the right phrase for it: "Their heart is as fat as brawn" (Ps. 119:70). It is this fatal egocentricity which we accurately label *original sin.*

It starts early. Before long, a newborn baby will be aware that a cry can bring someone to his side, for food, for comfort, for reassurance, for companionship. The universe out there responds to his initiative. So initiative begins and is developed. "We know you. We partied with you because we thought you were our type. We thought you were fun to know. *We* had decided, in other words, that your presence among us was a pleasure. We saw you on our territory teaching those who stopped to listen. That does not mean *we* stopped to listen. All it means is that we were aware of your being around and useful for other people. Not necessarily for us. The lower orders, they need to be taught." How patronizing can you get? Even while you are anxious to squeeze through that narrow door, there still are traces of the *droit du seigneur* in our protests: from the high to the low. Complacency still!

If that is how we seek to establish our identity and credibility with the Lord who maintains, "I do not know where you come from"—"I can't imagine where *you* come from"—then we face the frustration Christ talks about: "wailing and grinding of teeth." For there is something inconspicuous and hidden about that narrow door. It is hard to discover, in the first place. It is obviously inconveniently located, secondly. And as you and I know only too well, there is a certain loss of dignity involved in negotiating an opening too narrow; as Christ says, there is a struggle. It has been made not for our ease and dignity of ingress. We cannot take it at a triumphant gallop, or even at a stately trot in a landau, like Andrew and Sarah York, after their Westminster Abbey wedding, sweeping through Admiralty Arch. There is a confrontation and discomfort involved. Christ uses the word for *agony.*

But what is worse is that the door gets shut and locked. There is exclusion. This is of all things the hardest to take. Final unsuitability. There is a terrible finality about which Christ speaks. He talks of the master of the house having got up to lock that door (Luke 13:25). He talks of people still considering that they should not be excluded, who think they should be on the inside for what is taking place there. Preachers can preach until they are blue in the face about the mercy of God and still never succeed in conveying its vast breadth, its eternal dimensions. But there is still Christ's mention of final unsuitability, and I cannot stand here and attempt to diminish what he says or tailor what he says to fit our size and figure. I could wish that somewhere in Scripture there were evidences of a Divine relenting—a sort of back door for people frightened into getting their act together. But there is nothing by way of a crumb of comfort to offer. That door can be shut. And people will shout through the keyhole, "Sir, let us in!" (Luke 13:25). And they do not get in. They are, in Christ's own words, "thrown out" (Luke 13:27).

But who are they? Who are the people who somehow get in? Not merely the saints and heroes of the faith, the Abrahams, Isaacs, and Jacobs of this world, all the prophets of the church's history, as Jesus says, but the unknowns, from outside the bonds of family allegiance and faithful adherence—Easterners, Westerners, Northerners, and Southerners, unnamed, unknown, unrecognized, unsuitable, unconnected, unself-satisfied, but with a sense of need, with an infinite desire. They are the ones who will be satisfied with nothing other than companionship with their Creator and Redeemer. They will go through hell and high water to find him, will suffer the agonies of the damned, disappointment, rejection, and the catcalls of the chic, the successful, and the busy. They are judged unprofitable, perhaps unemployable, with priorities which are a puzzle to the wise and clever. There is a peculiar, maddening waywardness about God and the effect he has on people, so that what we, with our scale of priorities, can hold to be first, for some reason God places last. And this extraordinary turning upside down of comfortable human assumptions makes him a doubtful companion in the horse races of our complacent lives. Never bet, with him around. He produces winners with no recognized pedigree, with odds a million to one against; the utterly unexpected, the last one in the world we would choose. We know he does this. We have seen it happen and we can find no explanation that can account for it.

Nor can we confidently name the losers. He is not disposed to disclose specific prior information. All he does is warn us not to assume too much, not to trust too completely in the racing form we have in our hands, drawn up for us by knowing experts. Perhaps the assumption that people are out to *win* something may be the cause of the trouble. There is a certain naiveté, a certain unawareness of certain issues in the lives of those who come across that narrow door. They are not out to win something for themselves, but to find the beating Heart in which they can lose themselves and their own in the one Divine Heartbeat. They are the ones of whom Christ says: "Blessed are the poor in spirit, for theirs is the kingdom of heaven," or as the New English Bible translates it: "How blest are those who know their need of God." They are people who know they are nothing, who have nothing of consequence, who do not resent or count what others have, things which seem so fulfilling and important to them. They are the ones who travel light, and do not "make covenants with death," as Isaiah says, relying on their own wit and wisdom and resources of cunning and manipulation. They are the childlike, trusting souls for whom if they have God they have all they can desire, and other considerations leave them cold. They know their need of God.

And that narrow door, which permits no hand baggage, much less a porter panting behind with trunks and hat boxes, that narrow door through which they come singing

Nothing in my hand I bring;
Simply to thy cross I cling . . .

is just broad enough for the upright of the Cross itself bearing a body; the Cross Christ tells will be ours in the struggle: always with some loss of our dignity and impregnability involved. It will involve perhaps a personal grief, a crushing anxiety, a sickness of which the issue is only to welcome death as a friend, a loss, a blow, a burden unsought when, with nothing of ourselves to help ourselves, as the old Collect says, we are left naked for grace—God's life—to clothe us, yet singing all the while:

Now with gladness, now with courage
Bear the burden on thee laid,
That hereafter these thy labors
May with endless gifts be paid
And in everlasting glory
Thou with brightness be arrayed.

So You Think You Are the Salt of the Earth?

WHEN Christ declares, "You are the salt of the earth," he is not paying us a compliment. He is laying down a challenge. He is putting us on our mettle. He is displaying that astringency in his character and personality which some folks could not take. So they left him in droves because what he said was too hard. When he calls us special, watch out. There is trouble ahead; his own trouble and some trouble for us, too, if we throw in our lot with him. The "salt of the earth" is not an accolade of approval, although we constantly use the term in that mistaken way. It is a warning of costly expectation, on his part, of us. For he is in the world to judge it, and his judgment of it is that the flavor has gone out of it. Something is missing. There is a lack. The taste and smell of God has gone out of it. It is no longer holy. It is no longer fresh. It appears fresh—its freshness attempts to be self-sustaining by artificial means, and there is apparent success, but the whole business will go bad before we fully know it. Salt is the answer, to restore the flavor, to preserve its wholesomeness, to cleanse and to disinfect it. But it is used up in the process, and the uncomfortable thing, the disturbing thing, about being told by Christ that you are salt is that you are being told you will be used up, sacrificed, in the process of furthering the Divine purpose, of restoring the taste of Godliness, the odor of sanctity, and all this in the unpalatable and stale predicament the world has got itself into.

And here comes the crunch. What Jesus is talking about in this parable is your attitude toward self-preservation. You will remember that he goes on to say in his Sermon on the Mount: "You are salt to the world. And if salt becomes tasteless, how is its saltness to be restored? It is now good for nothing but to be thrown away and trodden under foot" (Matt. 5:13). He is saying that unless you are prepared to be used up like salt, absorbed like salt, to become nothing, like salt in the process of purifying, cleansing, preserving, bringing flavor back into a world which has lost its holy taste; if you sit there knowing that this is what you are meant for and refuse to allow yourself to be used by him, then the reason for your existence in his ministry to the world ceases: you take your place as road material, the useless dust for the unheeding traffic of history's purposeless meanderings. So it is that the truth of Christ's saying comes to life and light; that he who seeks to save his own life shall lose it.

But he is saying more. He says that there is a danger that this *will* happen. You can lose the very quality which he can use for his Divine purposes; this distinctive, redemptive ability he imparts in you *can* be squandered, dissipated, reduced to ineffectiveness, and all the potentiality for assisting in everything, refreshing the world, *his* world, recreating it in his desire to "make all things new" can disappear. Do you recall the evangelist Matthew's remark of pathos in the ministry of healing and comfort Christ was bringing to Galilee—"There he could do no great work because of their unbelief" (Matt. 13:58)?

For unbelief is at the bottom of this. Sure it is that no one will make an investment of anything if they have not committed themselves heart and mind to the enterprise. Get married without the heart-certainty that life is intolerable to contemplate except with your beloved at your side to face the years, and the seeds of marriage are being sown on stony ground. There has to be commitment. There has to be conversion to the Lord who is here in the world to make it and all things new. This is why our faith and our love for him is crucial, and I use the term advisedly, for its roots are in the Cross itself. For was not Christ himself God's salt among us? Did he not restore to newness the Divine flavor in us? Did he not cleanse us, bringing humankind back to what it is destined to be and to enjoy, namely the likeness and the eternal companionship of the heavenly Father? To do this, he gave himself totally and poured himself out for love of us as the redemptive process he performed secures us for time and for eternity. We are to be the salt of the earth because he is first that salt for us.

That, then, is the theological setting, if I may so put it, to a situation we as Christians must take seriously. Our job is to assist Christ and to make all things new. We have in this task to restore a stale and jaded world which has lost its flavor, its newness, its *joie de vivre,* its sense of purpose, its self-respect, its self-knowledge, under a forgetful and fake wisdom and a shabby and superficial cleverness. For we have all the assurance of the badly educated. We fail to learn the lessons of history. Our unreflectiveness is seen in the way we treat people who are different from us in color, in class, in sexual preference, in creed, and in economic condition. Jesus is making us face this state of things, and in making us face it, makes us face the fact that there is no substitute for our self-giving.

But it is in secret, this self-giving, this salting. It is hidden and it is small, for grains of salt are tiny things, contemptuously little and beneath the notice of the busy and the self-important and self-centered. Listen to what Christ has to say about this. He gives us two important clues about self-giving, not long after his warning to us about the salt, and not placed together coincidentally; they are part and parcel of each other: "When you do some act of charity, do not let your left hand know what your right is doing; your good deed must be secret, and your Father who sees what is done in secret will reward you" (Matt. 6:3-4). "When you pray, go into a room by yourself, shut the door, and pray to your Father who is there in the secret place; and your Father who sees what is secret will reward you" (Matt. 6:6).

This secret of self-giving, this salting, is in the setting of two costly areas: sacrificial, personal generosity, parting with what you treasure most, and doing it under the cover of discretion so that it goes from you unrecognized and is received from a source unknown to its recipient; and, second, parting with your most treasured heart-possession, your pride, in praying for the uncongenial, for those who have given you cause for hurt, for disappointment, for resentment and for self-justification. These secret sacrifices, generosity of hand and generosity of heart, are the constituents of the salting, the cleansing, the restoration of the Divine flavor of a world made tasteless, stale, and second-rate.

But it is precisely in these two areas that there appears a threat to our self-preservation. You give yourself sacrificially in a thousand private ways—and by doing so in secret you become vulnerable to misunderstanding or to rejection. The recipient may not be sure of the source, or may even resent the source of the charity. You pray—and you open yourself to the possibility of stagnation in prayer, a sense of the absence of God whom you wish to address, and whom, for some dark and mysterious reason, you somehow cannot contact. You become vulnerable to disappointment because your prayers are not being answered as you may think you have the right to expect. You pray, and your impatience may get in the way.

But still, you are *required* to be salt to the world, stemming from your belief in him who is humankind's salt, our purifier, our preserver, our healer: "O taste and see how gracious the Lord is!"—as Habakkuk knew and could declare in his discovery and pledge of undying faith with which his prayer ends:

Though the fig tree do not blossom,
nor fruit be on the vines,
the produce of the olive fail
and the fields yield no food,
the flock be cut off from the fold
and there be no herd in the stalls,
yet I will rejoice in the Lord,
I will joy in the God of my salvation.

Hab. 3:17-18, RSV

Eagles of the Word

PETER SHAFFER, the playwright, has something on Broadway which is busy blowing the minds of everybody who sees it: *Amadeus,* a remarkable story of Mozart's life—and death—through the eyes of Salieri, his self-confessed murderer, and the self-confessed monarch of musical mediocrity. We watch with dismay as Mozart bursts into the court life of Vienna, and transfigures the poor little *March of Welcome* which Salieri, as the resident composer, has cobbled and ground out, into a sparkling rivulet of sound, tumbling and catching the light like diamonds thrown into the air. Without effort, without false modesty, Mozart speeds through the musical firmament with sure strength, his lively intelligence and sheer genius shattering poor Salieri who sees his position as Imperial Kapelmeister threatened. Desperately he recognizes his own mediocrity for what it is, and hates himself and this young eagle for it all. He hates God the most for causing it.

That creativity, that resented gift of imagination in the soul of another, that spark of the Spirit of the Creator-Lord is something we can well ponder over at the Feast of Pentecost when according to Christ's own promise his Spirit is imparted with its myriad gifts upon his disciples. Their first discovery upon receiving the Spirit was a particular sort of *creativity;* they found they were able to communicate as they had never been able to before. They were manual workers, not word makers. They were forgiven cowards, not heroes with exploits to recount. Yet thus began the transformation of a craven pack of quarrelsome, unintelligent, utterly mediocre and enthusiastic anti-intellectuals into eagles of the Word "as the Spirit gave them utterance." Imagination, theirs and their hearers, took flight as they conveyed that Word to a waiting world.

It is a marvelous story, the account of Pentecost; the story of an explosion into our world—and its applications for us are legion. Even here in Manhattan, week by week as a preacher I have the task of sharing with a group of highly educated and, in some cases, learned souls who want to love Christ and to worship Christ and to allow him to live with us in a world which distrusts genius, is suspicious of excellence, though often it cannot recognize it, and resents it when it does so. A world of mediocrity in moral aspirations as in all else, preferring rabbits to eagles in all aspects of professional life, learning, and the arts, cowardly in holding fast that which is good, as St. Paul reminds us to do, and content to cower and mutter at those who refuse to accept mediocrity of standards in anything at all.

Yet there are those brave souls, thank God, who have a flame of fire in their minds, that majestic torch of *imagination.* Make no mistake about it: often it is too hot to handle, it burns and singes the whole of you with an uncomfortable energy that sets you apart, apart from the Salieris of this world, who for comfort's sake have committed the sublime treason of glimpsing excellence and settling for the second best. That priceless gift of God the Creator, that portion of his own creating spirit, this gift of imagination, is part of the love which truly "makes the world go round," constantly being renewed, refreshed, relit by that energy, "unresting, unhasting, and silent as light." And it is your heritage by your baptism to be offered a portion of it, and your duty to seek to exploit it, despite the fact that you will be labeled arrogant, elitist, perfectionist, and a traitor to much that others with whom you come into contact give their allegiance. Do not be dissuaded when eagles' wings are offered to you, their pinions are fastened to you. Of course I should perhaps warn you to fasten your celestial seat belts, if I may change the metaphor, for you are in for a rough ride.

The ride is through the firmament of creativity. There are constellations as yet unexplored, and waiting to declare the glory of God in every facet of his diamond existence, in the arts, in learning, in serving and in "maintaining the fabric of the world" as the ancient Scriptures describe the work of justice to be done, the work of liberation to be done—liberation of souls, of minds, of hopes for a place in the sun. There are works of mercy to be accomplished. There are hungers to be fed. There are wounds to be healed. There are bitter prejudices and foul-smelling memories to be made sweet, and hopes restored. And, yes, this also has to be said, there are souls to be saved. Not merely conversion to the true and living God, but our souls need also to be saved from self-satisfaction, self-absorption, self-justification, self-aggrandizement, and self-pity. We need nothing less than salvation from all the messes that self-ism creates and the disorders which the old Adam in us procreates: pride, greed, the ambition which should be made of sterner stuff—nobility, and the envy of that miserable Salieri.

There is so much to be done. There are so many places for it to be accomplished, if only souls would use their eagles' wings and fly with imagination and clear-minded courage.

And this goes for the use of imagination in our worship, too. At its best, worship is the foretaste of heaven, where as St. Augustine tells us:

> *We shall rest and we shall see*
> *We shall see and we shall love*
> *We shall love and we shall praise*
> In finem sed non infinem—
> *In the end that is no end.*

So wonder and adoration have their part in worship, and the preparation for it and the conduct of it require the use of the imagination, for the imagination has to be called forth in it, the self has to be left behind so that we can be "lost in wonder, love and praise." Thus, self-consciousness is alien to the best worship, where the soul can soar on eagles' wings.

But the greatest of the eagles are the humblest of people, deep down. I call to mind John Reith, the founder of the BBC in the 1920s in London.

He *looked* like an eagle, his war-scarred Scotch face betraying a tough Presbyterian cast of mind, as he towered at six-foot-five or six above lesser souls like me. A fire burned within him, unquenchable, a fire of a vision for bringing to a nation an emerging form of communication, the radio. He sped ahead of his fearful companions, sure-winged, his imagination showering sparks as he flew, a trail of stars as his genius pursued his vision. Relentless, demanding, judgmental at times, impatient at others, he drove himself and those who caught his spark and shared his vision into an accomplishment of worth beyond all telling. He yearned for decency, he yelled for integrity. He never stopped. He risked everything. What made him risk it was his faith. Like a child, he had the gift of silent wonder. His piercing eyes would soften as he would listen and think and read and pray and worship. He had wonder. He loved God. He was, as he used to admit to me, a cheating lover of Christ—he often, so often, failed in what he knew he must be and must live up to. But this capacity to wonder both softened his hard-skinned sins, and they were many and clamant, and strengthened his pinions, so that he flew tirelessly, looking, noticing, seeking for ways to make things better, and to make them best. For God. *For God.* I think of him as I think of those who responded with magnificent courage to the challenge of a poem by Lindley Williams Hubbell in his anthology *Dark Pavilion:*

> *Dare to be lost,*
> *However bleak the cost;*
> *Let your soul shelter no desire*
> *Save to be pierced with steel*
> *and burned in fire.*
>
> *Fear but this thing:*
> *that you should turn to rest*
> *Safe but unblest;*
> *Rather suffer this,*
> *Choose the abyss.*
> *There is no soul*
> *that in this torment dies*
> *Would have it otherwise.*

For everyone I could name, others will spring to mind, who are courageous, energetic, gifted—and humble with the gift of their imagination to wonder and to worship in awe of the Creator and Redeemer with whom a thousand years are but as one day, himself a source of all light, all life, all mystery: the hidden God who only hides himself in order to make himself known through our discoveries of him in other people and in great events, in marvelous music—yes, and in terrors, too, when "the nations furiously rage together" and violence stalks the earth, and blood and tears fall and the cries of innocent sufferers are heard. He reveals himself when senseless fools seek immortality through murder and popes and poor folk alike are victims to the lust of death and fear. When the world appears to be on fire, there, in the crucible of suffering, walk those who walked in the ancient Scripture story of Nebuchadnezzar who threw three godly men into a fiery furnace: "four men walking about in the fire free and unharmed; and the fourth looks like a God" (Dan. 3:25).

We are told in the Scriptures that those with ears to hear must hear. And the same must be applied to the eyes of the imagination: that they who have eyes to see must look to see. These imaginative souls on their eagles' flight will look into that fiery furnace of humankind's mindless violence and hate in the world of suffering, and though it burns their eyes to look, sure enough in the whitest of the heat they will discern the Son of God, walking free and making his presence felt and his being disclosed for sufferers and for the sensitive alike to experience.

It is not a pleasant sight. It is a searing experience. The cost of it and the pain of it are part and parcel of being human with the gifts from God to carry, for they are a royal burden. All the great souls have felt this pain, have borne this burden, have been all but blinded by that heat as they looked down from their eagle-flight, as they strove to discover, and to create, and to transfigure, and to reach for the dawn of excellence and truth of whatever form their quest took them. All dared to be lost: their souls sheltered no desire save to be pierced with steel and burned with fire.

This is why those souls eschew in their creativity a religion of little books or of little men. They scorn fundamentalism, and the fear which underlies a coward's thirst for the waters of authoritarianism. With that great philosopher and writer and priest Austin Farrer, whom I knew at Oxford thirty years ago, they would agree that there is nothing more deleterious than a faith which discourages you from having to *think*. For they would tell you not to be frightened of heresy—to risk heresy, rather than the unimaginative and constipated living of a bland faith with all the answers in neat packages from an urbane teacher, a little man or a little book. *Dare to be lost* to orthodoxy, for if you strive for the truth, the truth shall make you free. For it to liberate you, it must first find you. It will. For he who is the truth is the great Shepherd of the sheep who comes to "seek and save *that which is lost.*"

Of that gift of the imagination, vouchsafed every baptized child as a spark of the Spirit of the Creator-God, with which in worship and work you wonder and adore, and rise up on eagles' wings to discover and to create new things for him—of that great and glorious gift, a royal burden to be sure, the old hymn has something to tell us:

Now with gladness, now with courage,
Bear the burden on thee laid,
That hereafter these thy labors
May with endless gifts be paid
And in everlasting glory,
Thou with brightness be arrayed.

So You Think You Know?

I had a boss once whose greatest compliment for anyone was that she or he "knew what they were talking about." *That* set them apart from the pretentious and the exaggerators and those boring people who think they are the authority on every subject under the sun; the know-it-alls, the dogmatists, the smart alecks, and the opinionated. My employer was a holy man who had no small talk. But let him meet a person, young or old, who knew what he or she was talking about and the old boy was all attention, courteous, humble, and eager to listen. I have seen him on a sofa rapt in conversation with my youngest curate to the fury of others who imagined he would be better employed engaging *them* in conversation. But it was no use. He had struck a vein of gold in the young priest's mind and he was busy mining it, oblivious to the important, the self-important, the grand, and the great who were longing to have the same fuss made over them.

The biggest stumbling block for Christian souls is the failure to realize how little we can possibly know about Christ. We talk as if his life and his person were an open book. We talk as if we know all there is to know. We make confident claims about him and we harness him to our side, we link him with *our* projects, we claim him for *our* politics, we think of him as a partner in *our* prejudices, we use his name as an umbrella for our vendettas, our vengefulness, our personal crusades against people and causes we despise or distrust or disavow. We are self-professed past masters, experts, authorities on the person and work of Christ, and because we are, we are in the mess we are in. So, on one hand, some good and earnest Christians claim infallibility in the church's teaching and in certain pronouncements. On the other hand, some good and earnest Christians fall into the error of thinking that their interpretation of Holy Scripture is the only interpretation, and we are faced with the unthinking, anti-intellectual, and unscalable wall of fundamentalism, one of the biggest dangers to true religion the Christian world has ever to meet. And on yet another hand, we see some pulling Christ into their political camp and we have the phenomenon of the Moral Majority—to my mind neither moral nor a majority—which judges harshly and if unchecked could employ spiritual blackmail. Have these Christians never learned any lessons from the history of the Crusades and their extravagances, or the Spanish Inquisition and its cruelties? Or from the Elizabethan Star Chamber and its tortures? From Oliver Cromwell's brutal Roundheads who could smash the beautiful painted glass in every window of Lambeth Palace Chapel, my old home, and stable their horses in that holy place, ripping the lid from the tomb of a saintly archbishop and throwing his poor bones on the dunghill, making martyrs of both their lawful King Charles and of his archbishop, William Laud? We have seen the Ku Klux Klan's misuse of the sacred symbol, the sign of our salvation, the Cross from which our Savior hung, the sign of God's reconciliation with sinful humankind, as a sign of terror to black people as it burned on their property, a blasphemy and an outrage to every civilized Christian heart and soul who beholds it. Have these people never learned any lessons? They talk as if they know when, in fact, they know pitifully little.

Let those people take heed whose certainty about human rights spills over into the realm of putting Scripture to rights according to the light they think they have received when they rewrite it, desexing it. Leave it to biblical experts, I say. You would not thank me as an English citizen for attempting to rewrite your national anthem to accommodate my monarchist views. I should be a fool to try it and even more of a fool to hope you would swallow it. I claim to have the right to get just as cross at people who want to change God's Father-image to something else. Who do they think they are? I was just as annoyed at that wonderful bishop and pope, Paul VI, whom I knew a little and admired much for his kindness to me in 1966, when he removed St. Christopher and England's patron saint, St. George, from the list of saints because of doubts concerning their historical veracity. The truth is that St. George will be honored long after that dear pope's name, Montini, will be forgotten, or mistaken for the name of a cocktail.

People can be too certain about things. They talk as if they know. No. The fact is, we do not know as much as we think we know. Who says so? Christ says so. And we hear him say so in the Scriptures, when he says: "*No one knows the Son but the Father,* and no one knows the Father but the Son and those to whom the Son may choose to reveal him" (Matt. 11:27).

Now this is very sobering. It does us no harm to have our ignorant enthusiasm and certainty challenged and put into its proper place. We are not as smart as we think we are. It makes us realize that our explanations of what God is and does in the person of his Son Jesus Christ have to be respectful *and careful.* We must not make God in our own image. We have no right to be familiar or publicly cozy with God. A wise priest once said in the pulpit of my church in New York: "God is not the guy next door and we had jolly well better not forget it." We have our Lord's own warning; his warning and his guidance. We can be certain of one thing: that the *truth* about God is conveyed to us at Christ's initiative and only to those to whom the Son may choose to reveal the things of God. I am content with that. He has, in fact, been very generous and giving with us. He has shown us the Father in himself. Archbishop Michael Ramsey, the hundredth Archbishop of Canterbury, coined this perceptive phrase: "God is Christlike, and in him is no un-Christlikeness at all." He has given us the church, himself living in the lives of folks who believe in him and want to love him and know him. He has given us the Sacraments, when his life comes to us in the fullness of its power to help us "attain to the measure of the stature of the fullness of Christ," as St. Paul describes it. He has given us his word in Holy Writ, often hard to understand, to be sure, for his example and his teaching need the innocence of children to appreciate them. He has given us and still continues to give us the companionship of the saints who pray for us, and angels to bring us awareness of his nearness. And he has planted upon earth in every generation and in every race and tongue souls who reflect him in the myriad aspects of his holiness by theirs; saints alive, known and unknown, whose lives shine as lights in a dark world and bring his reality in their flesh and blood, in his courage which they display, in his patience, his love, his sufferings, his wisdom—in every conceivable situation, in every conceivable predicament, at all times and in all places, from all ages and to the end of time.

So with us, but not and never as a private possession. It is for *him* to possess us. It is for us to adore him, not to attempt to fence him in to the limited territories of our blinded sight. He is not as we think he is. Why, we do not even recognize him when we stumble across him, shining through the eyes of the poor and the unacceptable around us! He wants to make himself known; but on *his* terms, not ours, and he will do this when he sees we are open, and waiting, and humble enough not to think we deserve that glimpse.

"No one knows the Son but the Father." It is a healthy reminder. All we can do is to hope for a glimpse, and to be alert, "for ye know not the day nor the hour when the Son of Man cometh." But a glimpse is enough, this side of life's river. For we are promised, those of us who try to love him, the full disclosure only on that far side, where there is no more sorrow, nor crying, when he shall have wiped away the tears from every eye, to gaze upon that unveiled face, and in the glory of it and in the joy of it, in St. Augustine's words,

> *We shall rest, and we shall see,*
> *We shall see, and we shall love,*
> *We shall love, and we shall praise,*
> In finem sed non infinem—
> *In the end that is no end.*

Only then shall we know, because we shall know as we are known.

Keep Your Head, and Don't Forget to Disbelieve

KEEP your head, and don't forget to disbelieve." That was a piece of excellent advice I was given in classical Greek as a child. It comes from the pen of Epicharmos. It does not conflict with the Christian attitude to faith, either. We were given heads to keep, brains to think with, rational qualities to exercise and train like the rest of the endowments which make us who we are. We are *meant* to question things.

I remember once talking to a man on the very edge of success. He was, I am glad to say, at the threshold of a breakthrough in his creative life when he may well become famous and his name a new star in the firmament of the theater. He was about to be recognized, not by good fortune but by reason of his hard work and extraordinary gifts. He was twenty-seven, and brought up as a Roman Catholic until his questing mind refused to be satisfied with the answers the nuns gave to his questions at school, until there began to be for him a *credibility gap;* an unwillingness to accept formulae that were inadequate *for him,* intellectually thin, and to his mind self-serving. He came to St. Thomas, drawn possibly by the music and by the fact that the word had gone out that the clergy worked hard at their preaching.

When we talked together, he honestly listed his doubts, large areas of the faith where he was unsure, and he asked if with the doubts he had he could be of any value in the congregation. For every one of his, I told him, there were hundreds, thousands, more.

What does Buechner say? "Doubts are the ants in the pants of faith."

Recall Jonah praying from the belly of the whale which had swallowed him, and Peter jumping off the boat to run to Christ across the waters of the lake. Neither event perhaps all that easy to swallow! Yet events like these in the Scriptures can open up the whole subject of your faith's foundations. Would you consider your neighbor to be less of a Christian if she or he were to confess to you that in the scale of gospel importances and priorities being swallowed by a whale and walking upon water were irrelevant? Does your faith *depend* upon such things? For some, it does.

There are many good and holy people who believe such things without question. We saw the occasion when Southern Baptists affirmed the literal inerrancy of the Bible. I have seen, as a member of the Executive Committee of the American Bible Society, managers request the resignation of one of our translators after he had aired his views and doubts about the fundamentalist approach to Scripture, views which offended and angered many customers of the Bible Society. There is an area of sensitive soreness among Christians, a capacity for anger and insecurity which disturbs me and many of us. The fundamentalist approach to Holy Writ, while brave and utterly sincere, can often get in the way of itself. So I am fairly certain that St. Paul himself, with his classical education, might have been aware of that axiom in Platonic Greek: "Keep your head and don't forget to disbelieve." Aware of it and approving of it, with that questioning, restless, courageous mind of his, proving all things, as he himself advises his readers to do. No, there are dark shadows in fundamentalism which our church has recognized and rightly warns us to remember. The church tells us that to equate truth with precision is to limit truth to the confines of the scientific approach, when there are other approaches, equally valid. Truth can come through poetry, through music, through any of the arts as through the sciences, and God will not be "cribb'd, cabin'd, and confin'd" in the revelation of himself and his love in his Son Jesus Christ by one channel only. Often it is a channel dug by one set of people, dug to their depth, dug to their narrowness, dug to their measurements as to the right direction toward a cistern of their own design. You simply cannot put away your thinking cap to stand bare-headed before the Bible. It has a million ways—God has seen to it—of declaring the truths about himself, through history, through folklore, through cultic dance songs and battle cries, through erotic love poetry and through earthy jokes, through cynical assessments of human accomplishment, through gloomy predictions about humankind's fatuousness, through verse and through interminable genealogies, through tales twice told and through events recounted which contradict themselves, convict themselves by condoning base human motive and praising human cruelty, sharp practice and treachery. A million ways, ways apprehended by greedy sinners, liars like you and me, making up what we do not know, exaggerating and ducking under what is politely called poetic license, to tell some aspect of the work of God, the ways of God, the tenderness of God, the judgment of God, the vigilance of God, among us. And the miracle is that God uses it all, and causes his light to shine. The final effect of it all is a vast treasure house of different coins, some of the purest gold, others alloyed so as to be almost worthless. Did not Luther attribute the Letter of James an "Epistle of straw"?—contributing to an immeasurable fortune available to us to draw upon till time shall last—*the knowledge and love of God and of his Son Jesus Christ our Lord.*

Because this is so, we are required to think. The worst service I or any other preacher or teacher of God's Word could ever perform is to persuade you not to think. There is nothing more harmful to the human soul than a religion which discourages you from having to think for yourself.

So let us think about what Jonah said, and Jesus said, and Peter said. For in what they are saying, they use the setting as a jewel for God's revelation of himself, and the two stories, side by side, can help each other rather than hinder belief. Jonah prays; and curiously it resembles the Psalm: "Save me, O God; for the waters are come in, unto my soul. . . . I am come into deep waters, where the floods overflow me" (Ps. 69:1-2, KJV). In Jonah's words, "Thou hadst cast me into the deep, in the midst of the seas; and the floods compassed me about. . . . even to the soul" (Jon. 2:3-5, KJV). And then he mentions what it is all about—salvation. For he says, "yet hast thou brought up my life from corruption, O Lord my God" (v. 6).

Jonah is proclaiming the truth of salvation, that when there is nothing more that we can do, when our resources are finished, when *we are down and out,* God acts. Compared with this truth, the conviction that there is a loving, living God who rescues us from ourselves, from the mire and the messes we have made for ourselves, from the despair of selfishness lived to its rightful conclusions, from living with the consequences of our actions—rescues us, pulls us up and away, dusts us down, cleans us up, renews us because he remembers us, and loves us as he remembers; compared with the glory of this truth, does it really matter if the whale swallowed Jonah, or Jonah swallowed the whale? It is a legend, a myth, enshrining the glorious news of what God does: the good news of his love for us. *That* is the eternal significance of Jonah and the whale, and it is eternity that matters.

Now, let's look at what Jesus said and what Peter said, in the storm on the lake. Peter finds that his human resources fail him—he tries, but he sinks: "Save me, Lord." And Jesus saves him: "Jesus at once reached out and caught hold of him, and said, 'Why did you hesitate? How little faith you have'" (Matt. 14:31). "Save me, O God; for the waters are come in unto my soul." It is a story of salvation. Jesus comes, in the power of his endless life. He comes where he is not expected, when human hopes are dying and all that we can do is not sufficient. It is a marvelous story of the Divine intervention, and we *know* how this story encouraged the early church in the days of persecution and martyrdom, when in obedience to the Lord's command to his disciples, the church, the little ark, had set off in its stormy journey, only to discover that the risen Christ was with them through it all, conquering the waters of adversity, "riding upon the seas," risen, victorious, never to sink again in the floods of death.

Armed with *that* truth, the glory of it and the encouragement it brings, *of course* Christ's conquering the sea is understandable. It is a welcome and magnificent picture of resurrection triumph, for if God is with us, who can be against us?

Blind Obstinacy

FEW people in New York have not had the chance to buy a Cartier watch in the street from the top of a cardboard box, sold by the watchful Senegalese vendor. Or a Gucci bag. They look like the real thing. They have the same initials or the same name adorning them. The fact that they sell for a couple of dollars instead of hundreds is because they are not the real thing. Some can see this, others cannot. They buy. Tourists in Europe have been approached by postcard sellers and photograph vendors who in my experience have claimed to own the miraculous photograph of our Lord's face in a cloud formation. Some can't see it. Others can. They buy.

Often we see what we want to see, like those who hear what they want to hear. There is no doubt that predisposition governs and influences far more than we would care to admit. Predispositions distort. They can blind the truth. A "severe mercy" which the church bestows in Lent is the opportunity to try for as clear a view as we can have of our Savior. He himself asks the question: "Who do men say that I the Son of Man am?" He knows that who he is eludes many. He knows that what he says because of who he is confuses many, devastates some, angers others, gives others hope. He is aware that all around him people's predispositions govern their assessment of him. In how they see him, he knows how their souls are.

No one, ever, has been quite like him. This is part of the puzzle people find themselves in about Jesus of Nazareth. He says things and does things which are new to their experience. He knows this. Later he is recorded as saying that he comes to make all things new.

What he does, however, shocks them. He seems to ride the law. And as a rabbi, he is expected to explain it, not ride it. *This* rabbi says he is here to fulfill it, not to break it.

He begins by breaking it. It is a classic case: a healing on the Sabbath. The Scribes go to great lengths to explain this law, to define it to the last letter of the law. As with everything else in life, if you don't know when and where to leave well and good alone, you end up by spoiling the enterprise as well as making a fool of yourself. This point of the law had been chewed over until the issue was barely recognizable. You will recall that what Jesus had done was to restore sight to a blind man. St. John records this at length in his ninth chapter. Jesus had observed the ancient and deeply honored practice of using his spittle to make a paste or slurry of some earth. In his world and in his Galilean day, spittle was thought to have curative properties and medical treatises spoke of it with assurance and great respect. He had anointed the eyelids of this poor blind man. The man regained his sight and furthermore would not be silenced.

The great Bible commentator William Barclay has brought his extraordinary learning to this passage:

> By making clay, i.e., slurry, he had been guilty of working on the Sabbath when even the simplest acts constituted work. Here are some of the things which were forbidden on the Sabbath. "A man may not go out on the Sabbath with sandals shod with nails." (The weight of the nails would have constituted a burden, and to carry a burden was to break the Sabbath.) A man might not cut his fingernails or pull out a hair of his head or his beard. Obviously in the eyes of the law to make clay was to work and so to break the Sabbath.
>
> *Barclay,* The Gospel of St. John, Commentary, *pp. 44-45*

Perhaps it is worth interjecting here that in my own investigations into this business, I once discovered that the Pharisees had laid it down that you were not to eat an egg laid on the Sabbath because the chicken had transgressed the fourth commandment. Well, by the time things got to that stage of absurdity, the whole process needed to come under review. Christ was reviewing it.

Second, healing was strictly forbidden on the Sabbath. Only if there was a life-threatening situation were you permitted to do anything, and that was to keep the situation from getting worse, not to make him better. If you had a toothache you could not rub the tooth or suck vinegar through your teeth, the ancient remedy. Break your leg, and it had to remain unset. Sprain or dislocate your hand, and you were not permitted to pour cold water over it. The blind man was in no life-threatening situation. He would live. To heal him, Jesus breaks the commandment. There is no way around the rule, and Jesus knows it; about the use of spittle on the Sabbath, the law says: "It is not lawful to put it so much as upon the eyelids."

There. The law says it, and says it specifically. Jesus had driven a coach-and-four straight through the fence of that legal requirement. Do this sort of thing with impunity and the professionals who spend their working lives, their intellectual energy, their legal ingenuity on the consideration and argument of these matters will jump at you. They jump at Jesus as a flagrant scofflaw. What is worse, he has been committing these illegalities not out of ignorance, not out of irreverence, but out of conviction that he has a Divine mission. He dares to claim, "The Law says, the Law demands, but *I* say unto you. . . ." He is setting himself up in defiance to the law which made Israel recognizably different from all the other nations on the earth, which gave it its *particularity.* And he claims the sanction of God and the knowledge of God's ways and intimacy with the heavenly Father: "The Father and I are one."

There is no way, as the Pharisees saw it, that holiness and knowledge of God can go hand in hand with that attitude toward the sacred Law of Moses. Do not for one moment assume that the rest of the people in Palestine looked upon the Pharisees as flies in the ointment of their enjoyment of life, as cranky eccentrics, or as out of touch with the world. These learned men were revered, respected, listened to, deferred to. They kept the fabric of the nation together. They set the tone. They therefore called the tune. These men judged Jesus in the balance of legal rectitude and found him wanting. His credentials, they said, are worthless: "This fellow is no man of God: he does not keep the Sabbath" (John 9:16).

Here comes the problem which has dogged the world from that

day to this. The temptation is to admit only a recognizable God into your life. A recognizable God is a reflected God: the God of your own reflection. A God of your own size. A God of your own limitations. What the Pharisees were doing is still being done.

Permit a personal note. Once, some years ago, I was invited to preach for the Roman Catholic Franciscan friars in lower Manhattan on the Feast of the Annunciation of the Blessed Virgin Mary (March 25). It happened that one of the friars from that community regularly attended St. Thomas for Evensong and sat with the clergy. They were friends, and as friends they extended to me the ecumenical gesture of an invitation to worship with them and to say some words. But this invitation infuriated three good and holy people, not of their own congregation or parish, but ardent Roman Catholic anti-abortionists who saw the invitation as a scandal because the Episcopal Church has not taken the same anti-abortion stand as they had. They in fact did not even know what my views are. They had not even taken the trouble to ask. They tarred me with the same brush they perceive some extreme pro–abortion rights people are tarred with in the Episcopal Church. So they were intent on making the lives of the Franciscans miserable, and my life miserable, because they simply would not acknowledge that anything of God can come from a representative of a church which does not hold fast to a doctrine that complements their precise views of this grave moral issue. The life of an unborn child is a grave moral issue, and since God created it there has to be the tenderest respect for it. If they had asked me what I think I could have told them. But they had not. They berated the Franciscans. They berated me. They even wrote in protest to the Chancellor of the Archdiocese. They went further. They went to the pro-Nuncio in Washington. For they saw the whole ecumenical issue in the terms of interpretation of the abortion question. "This fellow is no man of God: he does not keep our anti-abortion requirement."

That is one small, insignificant, if annoying, application of the principle of prejudice. For prejudice it is. Here is another, and I want to refer to it discreetly. The shoe is on the other foot. I know an organization which accomplishes a lot for God. In some small way I am privileged to take part in its deliberations. Because of the wretched prejudice of some people whose goodwill it is necessary to cultivate and to continue to enjoy, the question of inviting a prominent Roman Catholic name to join forces to face a great need has had to be put on the back burner. "This fellow is no man of God: he does not keep the law which says God is Protestant, not Catholic." The narrowness and expediency of the policy needs to be reviewed in the light of Christ's decision to heal on the Sabbath.

The point is that Christ cannot be "cribb'd, cabin'd and confin'd" by legalistic assessment. If the Heaven of Heavens cannot contain God, as the Scriptures tell us, and if he is in himself the fulfillment of all law, then all law stands at a discount before him, all legal systems have to uncover their heads in his presence. He is simply not assessable, not measurable by the human yardstick. He will not be caricatured by cranky calculators of his person and work. He has come not to destroy the law but to fulfill it, he says. What the Divine fulfillment means in terms of our lives is simply beyond human imagination.

You chase Christ down the narrow alley of your own making and he will turn and confront you as he did Saul of Tarsus. Not to frighten you, but to look at you and make you see yourself in his eyes. Chase him down the abortion alley. Chase him down the feminist alley. Chase him down the chauvinist alley. Chase him down the sentimentalist alley, chase him down the pacifist alley. Chase him down the capitalist alley, the socialist alley, the alley of nostalgia, the alley of revolution; chase him down any alley between the walls of your own construction and fabrication, but before the end—for with him if not with you there is no end—he will turn and look at you. What you see in his eyes is yourself, judged as well as redeemed, with questions to be answered which you never guessed you would be asked.

Our Lady of Fifth Avenue

WHEN we dismiss the notion that in the light of this common day there could be what is called an *Age of Faith,* we forget the Age of Elvis Presley. Do you remember what happened around his tomb in 1987? A pilgrimage! A devotion! Souls felt drawn to his shrine, for that is what, in a crude and mindless way, his grave had become. People came from every place to see his grave; just to be there.

Compare and contrast with that a pilgrimage made by families of the St. Thomas choristers on tour in England gathered in one of the most famous places of pilgrimage in the medieval world. Thomas Beckett, the bad-tempered and violently courageous Archbishop of Canterbury, had been murdered in his own cathedral just after Christmas in 1170. Almost immediately he became a cult hero. Almost immediately people just wanted to be there, where he had died, where his body lay buried. His fame raced through Europe in days and weeks. I once looked in amazement in the great cathedral in Palermo, Monreale, in Sicily to see his standing portrait in the mosaics of the apse around the high altar—placed there, if you can believe it, to the right of the Blessed Virgin less than fourteen years after his death. Raised to the altars, held up to Christendom as a powerful representation of Christ's sufferings in half the time it has taken Elvis Presley's thirty-year cult to develop! That pilgrimage from Fifth Avenue was in Thomas's cathedral, not far from the place where his body had first lain the few days after his martyrdom, and where perhaps it may lie still in defiance of wicked King Henry VIII's direct command to burn the bones and scatter the ashes to the four winds.

In the undercroft, as they call the crypt, pilgrims to this day stand almost under the site of his shrine where the knees of millions of pilgrims have worn a declivity in the polished marble of the surrounding pavement during the four centuries that his devotion flourished. In the dim light of that undercroft you can see the statue of Our Lady, set high in the niche under the central arch. She holds her Blessed Son in her lap, quietly looking at him and beyond him to the faces of the people who approach him with their prayers. She is waiting, resting, ready, showing her Son to the world. Her face is calm and silent.

It so happens that her original statue disappeared in the fury of the changes wrought by overzealous and vengeful Christians at the Reformation. In the desire to reform, much cruelty, much vandalism, much spite, and much psychologically suspect hooliganism was cloaked in spirituality, leaving a trail of misery and injustice and robbery for the little ones of God's earth to cope with and to come to terms with. Many top people made what we now call a rip-off. The very top people made a gigantic rip-off. In the clamor of the changes, lovely things disappeared, and Mary's statue was one of them.

Her replacement, in my lifetime, is a treasure of Continental ivory. *She* also was stolen within the last decade. What we saw was her replacement, modeled and sculpted by a nun from a Contemplative Order, Mother Concordia. The Dean and Chapter had her placed there.

Now, mysteriously and inexplicably, more and more pilgrims are coming to this place to say some prayers, to kneel, to sit and look, to light a candle on the metal stands at the sides, near her, to bring their hopes and their dreads and their disappointments and leave them there as they pray to Christ and ask Mary's help with her prayers. It is a phenomenon we know about; it is a natural and human thing to do. If thousands can visit Elvis Presley's grave, is it so strange that many thousands more come to the Chapel of Our Lady Undercroft on pilgrimage at Canterbury? The place is coming back into its own as a shrine, having called untold myriads of souls to itself who feel the holiness of the place and the need to visit it. It is becoming a shrine. And people are claiming miracles performed at her intercession on their behalf. People are saying that things are happening there and that the Mother of the Lord has something to do with it all.

Has she? Is it part of the Christian experience to consider her? I frankly think it is and I commend the mystery to you. You cannot deny that I have history on my side.

Look at the earliest churches ever built. They were built in the basilica pattern, a building they were familiar with. The Romans were in the habit of building a large meeting room with a rounded apse at the end, for the throne or chair of the dignitary, or Caesar. That is why it is called a basilica: a place used by a king. The first churches were built on this pattern. In the top of the apse they placed a portrait of Christ, the King of kings, *Pantocrator,* usually a head and shoulders, holding the Gospels. Below him they portrayed his Mother, seated on a throne. Individual saints stood beside her: all were placed below the great picture of the victorious Christ. Inescapably the moral of the story makes itself plain. The Mother of God, they named her: *Meter Theou*. She has the place of honor under her Divine Son. She gave Christ birth, and bore him into the world of you and me, for you and me. There was no thought in the early church that by honoring Mary, despite would be done to her Son and Savior. Christ would lose no iota of worship for having his Mother honored in this way and it is a gross begrudging to think otherwise. What can make us uncomfortable—and rightly so—are the sentimental flights of fancy and the sugar coating of the enthusiasts who took her role out of all proportion to her human state of creatureliness, and tinseled her with quasi divinity. She must shudder at the attempt. In a seventeenth-century icon in my rectory, above the body of Mary on its deathbed, Christ her Son is holding her soul like a small child and taking it into heaven where all the apostle-saints, who knew her, are waiting with the angels to welcome her. It is a magnificent poem of a picture: a loving, unsentimental, generous attempt at portraying what the church has always thought about her departure from this earthly life.

Generous. If you were to ask me for a qualifying adjective, for a word which would encapsulate the concept of Catholicism, of which we as Episcopalians claim a legitimate and ancient part, it would be *generous.* Show me stingy Catholicism and we could find it is not authentic, somewhere. Have you never realized that we are Eucharist-centered in our church life because we cannot help retailing Divine hospitality—the foretaste of the heavenly banquet, with our ever-giving, ever-living Divine host wanting to feed and strengthen us?

So we welcome the place of Mary in the Divine scheme of things. If ever a person deserved our gratitude for what she has given to us all, this is the person, *Theotokos,* the God-bearer. Of course you can do without her. She would be the first person to agree, because she is the soul of unselfishness, of reticence. And she has been treated like that by people who profess and call themselves Christians since the Reformation. But look at those who never spare her a thought, or who are frightened or inhibited at the thought of welcoming her, talking about her, asking her to pray for them. Not very impressive, always, are they? Often they are quick to split up into quarreling fragments, and that is the misery and the curse of much Protestantism, cutting off its nose to spite its face. She makes no claims for herself; she never did. She employs no PR firm. The hearts of people who are grateful for her gift to us of the world's Savior—hers as well—are the earthly home she has. And the quiet insistence of people who own the faith of Jesus, who are committed to him, who know and love him—that quiet insistence on asking his Mother's prayers is showing in places like Canterbury Cathedral in the chapel dedicatd to her in the undercroft. Then there is Walsingham, where now hundreds of thousands of pilgrims annually wend their way to her shrine and where miracles have been attested in that holy little place, tucked into a remote village in Norfolk, where I have found much peace, much comfort.

My task here on noisy Fifth Avenue is to see that a widely balanced, full-blooded, wholehearted, generous, and biblical faith is taught and practiced, stretching the intellect, demanding upon the time and the minds and the self-giving of those who love Jesus, in worship, in praise, in sacrificial works of mercy. We need all the help we can get. New York needs a shrine; this crazy city needs such meeting places, silent and hidden. But frankly Elvis Presley's will not do! It may well be that a place the size of St. Thomas could do with a fine and austere representation of the Mother who gave him to us, as a reminder of the love she carries for us all, as a symbol of patient waiting and contemplation, and as a place of quiet access and constant readiness to show Christ to the world of busy business. So perhaps Our Lady of Fifth Avenue is not out of place.

And as he loves thee, Mother dear.
We too will love thee well,
And to His glory, year by year,
Thy joy and honor tell.

Divine Disobedience—*Saint Francis*

A young Franciscan in his brown monastic habit got into a train somewhere in England. Across from him sat a large man with glasses, reading his paper. He lowered the paper and looked at the Franciscan friar, up and down, from tonsure to the toenails sticking out of his sandals. "And what, may I ask, are you supposed to be?" "Polite," said the young friar.

This young man belonged to an organization founded on disobedience. But disobedience of a strange sort. Some eight hundred years ago, Giovanni Bernadone was born into a family that had plenty going for it—prosperous, well-thought of, hardworking. His father Pietro wanted, as all good fathers do, the very best for young John who blossomed, we are told, under the favored treatment he received from indulgent parents—well dressed, with a shrewd eye for the prettiest girls of the town and a tune in his head to sing to them, and "the usual store of wild Italian oats to be sown." The nickname *Frenchy* was given to him; he was a fancy young character who went off to the wars, fell off his horse and was captured as a prisoner of war by the German invaders. He came back from his prison in Perugia ill and tormented in spirit. He had seen something, been somewhere in his soul, unknown by and unsuspected by his family and friends. He had had a glimpse of what it meant and could mean to be poor. He was haunted by it, undaunted by it, burned to his depths by it. The defenselessness of the poor spoke words he knew had been spoken before and he knew who had spoken them. And he knew for sure that they were aimed at him and that they had found their target. He was speared like a flounder finally on February 24, 1208, when he heard the Gospel read at a Mass of Saint Matthias, and he made the change from hermit to barefoot preacher.

It had taken years. This was no lightning conversion of the kind some folks experience at a tent meeting. Sown into it were all the seeds of rebellion which flowered into Divine disobedience. The Scriptures record a lot about obedience and the prophet Ezekiel has several unpleasant things to say about rebelliousness. The story of St. Francis is the story of hilarious and holy disobedience, rebellion about the right things, obtuseness on eternal things. What are they? They are secrets until you discover the strength of defenselessness, the riches of poverty, and an utter nonchalance toward the serious matters of life like filial piety and deference, the keeping up of appearances, the adding of one cubit to one's worldly stature in an upwardly mobile society, and settling down. The world's generation of hippies could have had him as their special patron saint if only they could have appreciated what led him to do the things they thought they were doing and to live the life they thought they were living. But sadly few got it, and got it right.

Father knows best and threatens to put Francis back for another spell in the military to sort him out. Francis does what legions of youth in their near-twenties have done and leaves home for an unknown destination. He emerges from it convinced that he knows best and takes his cloth-maker father's wares to sell, plus horse, to give the proceeds for church-restoration purposes at San Damiano. Father takes him to court and Francis takes his clothes off and throws them to his father, and runs naked as a worm from his father's life.

Some story. Try and fit this into your conventional view of honoring your father and your mother. And then realize that Christ—whose obedience to the Father's will is lived out and died through and is the source of his eternal priesthood—realize that only the Christ who *is* the eternal *"life"* can say, "No man is worthy of me who cares more for father or mother than for me; no man is worthy of me who cares more for son or daughter" (Matt. 10:37). Here within the granite of the Gospel runs a line of lead, an impurity at first glance, a disconcerting contradiction, one of his uncomfortable words, to be sure, and not what we tend to think of him as saying.

It has echoes in something else that Matthew records: "I have come to set a man against his father, a daughter against her mother, a son's wife against her mother-in-law" (Matt. 10:35). Perhaps we can understand the mother-in-law bit, but we are not prepared to stand for the sundering of the closest possible family ties: a child with a parent, a husband with a wife; and not merely a sundering but an antagonism: Christ says, "If anyone comes to me and *does not hate* his father and mother, wife and child, brothers and sisters. . . ." "I have come to *set a man against* his father." He says it. You have three choices. Reject it. Water it down. Or somehow take it into account.

Reject it and you tailor the gospel to suit you, to fit you. You treat it as an overcoat to shut out drafts and storms which get to you. Water it down: call it a "rhetorical exaggeration." Is "Forgive your enemies" a similar rhetorical exaggeration? Water it down, which is what liberal Protestantism had done with it a couple of generations ago, calling sayings such as this *interimsethik,* Christ being under the impression that the world would end within a few years and thus legislating for an "interim period" before his final return at the end of this age. Do this and you proclaim a deluded Christ, you end up achieving what liberal Protestantism has wrought in this century, the fruits of which are the disillusionment of many of the young people for whom the "otherness" of God, the mystery of God, the majesty of God are so important. So not unnaturally they have turned to other methods of perceiving them, such as meditation methods from Eastern religions and hallucinatory drugs. They have explored and employed these in their disenchantment and disbelief with a dried-out and castrated gospel.

Or somehow take it into account. This terrible phrase—and it *is* terrible, it makes me fearful and frightened—has something to do with discipleship, with being a follower and a learner of Christ. It is an indispensable requisite for being a disciple. It is a *sine qua non.* Without this, "he cannot be my disciple." This dread condition, this inescapable price, this sacrificial cost is repeated three times. Christ is using a rabbinic method of emphasis. He hammers the nail of discipleship's price three times. After hating family, he goes on to include cross-carrying and renunciation of possessions. Setting a man against his father. There is such a thing as family idolatry. I give you four examples:

1. The family can be held up as a claim to be excused from the performance of valid duty. The family claims can be sheltered behind as a plea for not doing something you know to be right and urgent, not to mention kind and self-giving. People can plead family for not giving what perhaps they should to their church and to charity. Who has not heard the axiom, "Charity begins at home"? As with all true sayings and wise sayings, untruths can be spawned when they are used with a questionable motive.

2. The preoccupation with family can blind a member of it to reality, and the later cost to that family can be disastrous. You can persuade yourself that your husband or your brother is not an alcoholic when in truth he tragically is. You can resent and resist the suggestion of an outsider and spurn the offer of help for your family member. Is it not true that we can lose good and old friends who have perhaps summoned the courage to point out something about a member of the family that we do not wish to think about? "None of their business," we say, when an hour's recollection would overwhelm us with evidence that it *is* all too true.

3. Then there is the unhealthy obsession with family. A member of society who is perfectly reasonable about relationships he finds difficult with colleagues or partners in business, knowing that there is work to be done on these relationships and that he has to do his share, may leave all reason and resonableness behind on the outside of his apartment door, because inside, within the family, there is a mindless, never-ending, unreasonable feud and quarrel to which neither party will contribute any willingness to seek a reconciliation. As a pastor, I have listened to the latest round of battles in a family feud which has festered and fomented for longer than most of the family members could care to remember, and this from people who are intelligent with outsiders, generous in charity toward their neighbors, and altogether charming to their friends.

4. Finally, there is that pathetic reliance upon family history,

real or imagined, which is used to bolster up one's own inadequacies and *un*achievements. It stems from a sad discontent with life as it is, and a desire to impress, and so cheaply to purchase respect. It is more silly than sinful; it never achieves what it aims for, because genuine pride in one's family and wholesome respect for its history usually expresses itself in a desire to be of service, seeing it as an opportunity to do good for its own sake, from gratitude to a gracious God who is no respecter of persons.

But, hating the family? Does not that imply substituting one powerful emotional involvement for another? Hating *can* be obsessive, time-consuming, and even to some souls nourishing, in a terrible way. Can Christ mean this? Is he on the one hand demanding this attitude toward our own flesh and blood and on the other loving our enemies? What I suggest to you that Christ means is to see hating in terms of *a passionate desire to be free from any obsession* with the family's ties and claims, an obsession which shackles and breeds idolatry, where God is lost to view in the preoccupation with the family. So then there can be no using the family as a shelter and excuse for not being Christian, no using the family as victims for mindless and shameless rage and cruelty, no using the family to make other souls, in the words of Scripture, "small and of no reputation" as a means of shoring up the self-esteem of one's own.

Smash the shackles of family idolatry and you will love the members not less but more. You will be liberated by the clarity with which you see their claims in the pattern of Christ's claims upon us all. Christ knows that family idolatry is among the most powerful deterrents from discipleship. He has seen it. He has suffered from it. Listen:

> He was still speaking to the crowd when his mother and brothers appeared; they stood outside, wanting to speak to him. Someone said, "Your mother and your brothers are here outside; they want to speak to you." Jesus turned to the man who brought the message, and said, "Who is my mother? Who are my brothers?"; and pointing to the disciples, he said, "Here are my mother and my brothers. Whoever does the will of my heavenly Father is my brother, my sister, my mother." (Matt. 12:46-50)

Christ is asserting the necessity for recognizing priorities in any sort of relationship we care to have with him. You come on his terms, not yours. You learn family love from his relationship, from nobody else. It is a sharp lesson in the quality of detachment, and Pietro Bernadone thought his son a perfect fool for taking Christ seriously. But then Francis was a perfect fool. He was a saint.

Two Men Called Jack

OVER twenty-five years ago, when I was a curate, I had a friend called Jack. Jack was the proprietor of a sleazy shooting gallery and a slot machine dive on the boardwalk of the town I worked in. His language had a higher percentage of expletives than anyone I have known, before or since. He had a string of young ladies, but never a wife. He was unlettered, untidy, unlawful. And he had a heart of gold. He was humbly generous to the church, and also to the poor. He loved to travel. His imagination was stirred by the story of Pompeii. So to Pompeii he went, and he took great delight trying to shock me by what he had seen painted on the walls of an ancient Roman bordello. And then he surprised me: "I stood among them ruins, John, and cast my mind back to that civilization, how great it was. I looked up at them lovely buildings, and I felt bloody insignificant."

How very different from Little Jack Horner. Listen:

Little Jack Horner sat in his corner
Eating his Christmas pie.
He put in his thumb and pulled out a plum
And said, "What a good boy am I!"

And so it was that his journey into self-significance, smugness, self-assurance, and miserable bumptiousness had begun. It was the predicament of humanity; the infection, the disease which all human beings seem somehow to have within their systems, simply because they are human. Yet it is tragic, since being *really* human means to have the Divine spark shining: that fatal infection of self-sufficiency, self-love, which wars against that quality we call creatureliness, the awareness that we owe something, at least something, and in fact *everything,* to the God who loved us enough to make us. For someone had tended that tree which grew that plum, and someone had spent time cooking that pie, and God it was in the life first stirring in the seed from which the plum tree grew. But Jack was not to know, and apparently couldn't have cared less.

So the human predicament. It starts with us. We find ourselves fascinating. We start from there. And the pity of it is that we do not move much from that starting place. Self-centeredness—scarcely are we born before it appears, as any observant parent will have noticed. The world must move around *us,* folks must dance to *our* tune. But it does not, they do not, and trouble begins. The trouble with this kind of trouble is that having begun it is damnably difficult to stop. Our infantile egotism has time with all else to mature, and refinements come with the years. Some of us realize we are clever. Others of us realize we are beautiful. The luckiest of us realize we are both. Some with more of one than the other might plan to put the balance right. George Bernard Shaw, who was preoccupied with his own intelligence, once was having an affair with a beautiful woman who was very aware of her beauty.

"Let us produce a child," she said. "With your brains and my beauty the child would be the wonder of our time."

"Yes," said Shaw, "but what if she had *your* brains and *my* beauty?"

What of those who have neither? Along with all the machinery for encouraging vanity and narcissism in the beautiful and arrogance in the clever there is everything in the world to encourage a human soul to be resentful, possessive, cunning, greedy, domineering, downright nasty, and just plain selfish. No soul is immune to the human predicament, free from the temptation to self-centeredness of one sort or another. The machinery for it is here. It is here because we are here. It is the machinery of disorder, and disorder reflects the traces left by the devil who seeks to undo the gracious and patient work in us of a God of order in whose image we were lovingly created. It is subtle, this wrecking system, subtle and superbly inventive. It takes things and situations in which we are involved; it takes our predispositions and our attitudes, *all of which may be good in themselves,* and gives them a half-turn, a slight twist. And that is all it needs to render human activities self-directed, to reduce human situations into opportunities for exploitation, to make human endeavor calculating and self-aggrandizing, human hope into hope of gain. C. S. Lewis in *The Screwtape Letters* puts this point magnificently. The human predicament is the disorder in a personality called by theologians *Original Sin,* the sin of Adam, the sin of primary disobedience, the bias within us to prefer ourselves, to choose ourselves, to assert ourselves over those who surround us. For humanity was not meant to behave like this. The isolation which results, the isolation from the Creator, the growing sense of estrangement from him, the growing distrust of evidences of his existence in other people, is the tragedy of human history. Man was made for a happy companionship with his Creator who has left joyful signs of his interest in us in the world and in the people who surround us. We were not meant to have hearts of brick. Nor are we here to be miserably isolated from the people around us because of it.

I am convinced that there is a real necessity to repeat Christian teaching such as this. We need to be reminded gently, courteously, but firmly of our malady. For we immerse ourselves in crises of our own making; the newspapers deafen us with the roar of bad news and doom which stem precisely from that same predicament. When the profit motive becomes too important and large corporations resort to bribery in order to sell, what is that but human endeavor rendered calculating and self-aggrandizing? When Protestant murders Catholic in Ireland what is that but the tragic isolation of men from each other and both from their Creator? When judges are found to bend justice for political ends, and when we are prepared to spend hours looking at the idiot box, the television, to catch up on some trashy item of scandal, what are they evidences of but the wreckage caused by this old-fashioned Original Sin? Call it what you will. Dress it up in every fancy euphemism, but the fact remains that left to ourselves, *left to ourselves,* we have a capacity for spoiling and soiling what God has given to us. It is all a matter of many variations on the same theme song: Jack and his pie.

How true the words of the Collect: "Because through the

weakness of our mortal nature we can do nothing that is good without you." Back then to first principles, to the fact of our creatureliness because God is our Creator, the God who in an act of superabundant *joie de vivre,* of overwhelmingly happy love, made the world and us to share that joy, to spread that joy by letting the love he poured into us pour over into our surroundings and into the hearts of the people about us. For he wanted music to sound upon the earth he had made, the music of joy, a mighty orchestra of humankind's response and self-giving to him who had given it all to them in the first place. The secret he held and so much wanted men to find was in the love that, as the Queen said to Alice, "makes the world go round." That other Jack, for all his expletives, had come very close to just that secret.

And since we can choose to learn to look for that secret or to ignore the many hints and myriad clues to its discovery, God has taken a risk with us of such dimensions that only the deepest love on his part and most daring act of faith could think up: the possibility of our not returning it, of preferring isolation from it, alienation to it, the solitariness of self-sufficiency.

That is what he has done, and that is what we have done in response. But he still pours out his love on our fretful, irritable, self-concerned heads, and our alienation from him is thwarted by the gift of *himself* in his Son. "God commends his love to us in that while we were yet sinners Christ died for us." The Lenten exercises of self-discipline and denial are to help us better to contemplate the majesty of that picture. For on Good Friday our hymn will be

Look, Father, look on his anointed face
And only look on us as found in him.

Yet the church is wise in placing before Lent three Sundays in which are portrayed the whole great setting of the world God made and man's place in it and predicament upon it and God's answer. We are bidden to meditate on God's creation *before* we reflect upon our need for redemption. This concept, so vast, so staggering, and so compelling, has been explained in the words of a lecturer at Oxford (whom, as irreverent and ignorant undergraduates, we had written off as desiccated and irrelevant until we heard these words and marveled at their wisdom): "Get over the fact that God made the world and you can get over anything."

This is the truth which should shake us from our self-preoccupation, each sitting in our corners pulling out plums from our pie with never a thought for the might and majesty of that great Creator as we say what good boys we are: self-centered clever boys deaf to the voice of his calling, heedless of the myriad clues to his secret which he so longs to share.

So we approach the discipline of Lent best from its furthest gates with the prayer of Elisha for his servant. We need to make it our own. "Open my eyes, O Lord, that I may see" the glory of your created world and my place upon it—not an island, unto myself, but tied eternally in a kinship with humankind who share God's spirit and spark. In it teach me that to be myself I need not only myself but God, and my sisters and brothers with me; that from them I shall learn about this God; from them I can understand what the love is that God's Spirit sheds abroad; and that on the mean altar of my heart Christ's spirit alone can kindle his sacred flame of love which to God's glory will burn here and hereafter.

The Borrowers

SERMON racks at the backs of churches have seen their fill, I suspect, of efforts to expound the parable of the Foolish Virgins. They were foolish not for the fact that they were virgins as for the fact that they simply were not ready when the bridegroom came. It is the custom still in the East not to give a clear indication of the time, or even the day, when the wedding ceremony will happen. You have to go no further than the islands of the West Indies to realize that people can have different ideas about the importance of measured time—and still in some places in that ancient country of Palestine the bridegroom can appear and catch the bridal party napping. It is the sort of opposite to our song of the disconsolate bride: "There was I, waiting at the church, waiting at the church. . . ."

But an aspect of the parable waits for deeper thought—the words of those unfortunate women: "Give us some of your oil, for our lamps have gone out." Borrowing somebody else's oil. There are things in our lives which cannot be borrowed. You have all seen the television commercial in which that aging actor with an annoyed and irritated English voice says of the people who work at the investment firm of Smith Barney (which speaks also of its reputation): "We *earn* it." You cannot borrow a reputation. You have to earn it.

You cannot borrow a character, either.* Your character is part of you: it is the outward and visible sign of an inward spiritual condition. Your character may change only when you change. That is what redemption can mean: God making things right, God "making

*I have Dr. William Barclay to thank for this insight.

nice guys out of stinkers." But you cannot stay as you are and borrow a character and hope it will fit. Some people can be fooled some of the time, but it is highly unlikely in your life that all the people can be fooled all the time. To hope for a character that is, in effect, a disguise, borrowed clothes; to hope that we will be taken for something other than what we are is something we all dream about. Hypocrisy is part of the human condition. I suppose the first step to take in putting all this right, by God's grace, is to be aware that we do this. George Bernard Shaw was right when he addressed some seminarians: "Gentlemen, I am glad to be in the company of conscious hypocrites." Our Lord had something uncomfortable to say about old wineskins being borrowed to contain new wine. You cannot borrow a character. You want a new character? You must get a new heart first. That is biblical language. There are lots of references to our need of a new and contrite heart. Only then can you "grow into the measure of the stature of the fullness of Christ."

You cannot borrow life from anyone. Just as time and tide wait for no one, we all know what Christ has to say about the means we employ to borrow what is not ours to borrow: "By gaining his life a man will lose it; by losing his life for my sake, he will gain it" (Matt. 10:39). Christ's life. You cannot borrow Christ's life. You can be given it—but only by being willing to part with your own. His life is the resurrection life of the spirit, the life hid with Christ in God, the life of which Paul could say: "Nevertheless I live: yet not I, but Christ liveth in me." What you will bargain in exchange for your own is something incomparable, ineffably grander and greater than what you might hope to borrow. If you are afraid to grow old; if you are afraid to be alone, of being lonely; if you are afraid to die, borrowing will not help. Giving yourself to God will. Ask him to accept you and your fears and secret terrors by accepting him.

You cannot borrow someone's relationship with Christ. There can be no substitute for a personal relationship with God in Christ. You can immerse yourself in church and charitable activities; you can sew and polish with the altar guild; you can organize the ushers; you can be an efficient and informed vestryman; you can be a wizard with figures and a genius for organizing enterprises for the women; you can work in the soup kitchen projects or go among the poor in the various works of mercy the parish participates in. You can be philanthropic until it hurts; you can work your fingers to the bone. You can sing your head off on Sundays and pat the preacher on the head for telling you things you like to hear. You can lose yourself in all of this, give yourself, exhaust yourself. But it all can be borrowed oil if the oil of your own commitment to the one Person who makes all this make sense is not there.

At this point what I say may be dangerous. We must apply this principle to the mission and work of the whole church. If the church loses her nerve and is tempted to feel she has nothing more to say (and there have been times—we are possibly just emerging from one—when her theological priorities have become uncertain and the light of her faith is dimmed), she may turn to the world, what she may think wistfully to be the *successful* world, and say, "Give us some of your oil, for our lamps are going out." She may temporarily have lost her nerve; she may temporarily have lost her determination to preach Christ in the secular cities and among the titanic heights of urban conglomerations. She may think that she must retrench, close churches, bring everything up to date and up to taste, rid herself of what she sees to be eccentricity, adopt not merely the methods but the mindset of the secular trade. She may get itchy about communicating instead of listening a bit, assume that what will bring the future generations flocking through her doors will be a *reductio,* a reducing of the mystery of the faith like the virgin birth of Christ or his resurrection, downplayed, tailored to the twentieth-century sensitivities of the Western world, couched in secular technical language; this also is to be seeking borrowed oil.

If she finds the gospel with its challenge of daily cross-carrying and self-abnegation offends the precious and very successful psychology of selfism so that she longs to preach the importance of success and self-esteem and the power of positive thinking, then she is after borrowed oil, for she will search the pages of the Bible in vain for references to them. If she takes a political stance and tailors her preaching to fit it, if she fails to maintain stubbornly and courteously that worship is the paramount activity of Christians before all else, if she fails to remember that you do what you do because you worship what you worship, she is after borrowed oil. If she tries to convince the faithful not to think for themselves, to rely instead upon an infallible book or an infallible man, she is after borrowed oil. If, on the other hand, she hides behind ecclesiastical buzz words and shelters behind the safety of shibboleths; if she gives people outside her doors the impression that the church of God is some sort of club for the elite, the nice, the healthy, the sexually so-called orthodox, the respectable, the saved, she is in danger of being after borrowed oil.

For the fuel for the lamp of faith, like the flame of love, cannot be borrowed. There is no other way than through Christ and him crucified and risen and ascended, with whom we have an individual friendship through prayer and Sacrament. Having said that, there is one thing that can be borrowed, that you can ask to be given in loan: it is the power of the Holy Spirit of God, of Christ, the strength to go on uphill for love of him, to persevere, to pick ourselves up when we fall yet again, to hope and to strive for the dawning of the day when the bridegroom comes and when we shall recognize that wondrous face and see in his eyes the recognition of us, cleansed, welcomed, advancing from glory to glory in the praise and eternal worship of the God who loves us forever and forever. We sing of the Anointing Spirit. She wants us to borrow and to borrow and to borrow until the End—which is no end.

Noise in New York

THERE is much too much noise in New York. One Friday evening, as I was on my way to supper, the whole air was filled with the blare of fire engine klaxons as they raced up Madison and Park and from West to East. They were about their rightful business, to be sure, to save lives and to put out fires, and their warning noise needs to be louder than the thunder of Manhattan traffic. The point is that their din combined with the pounding of road drills, whose optimistic tradename, I noticed, was "Quiet-Flo," made life intolerable for passersby for the minutes we were experiencing it; surely as much a pollution as the dirt in the air and the contamination in the East River.

I remember that I had my afternoon in Central Park ruined one day some summers ago by some cretin with a radio as big as a suitcase blasting its inanities half a mile, and I was within yards. All I could do was to withdraw, deafened, defeated, and depressed, to some place where I could hope not to hear the noise which apparently pleased him so much. It was music, all right; but not the kind for parks, or me.

The truth is, as an article from a magazine sent to me by a friend says, some people need loud, insistent sound. "People . . . are conditioned to noise as a feature in life. It is reassuring phenomenon, evidence that they are not alone in the world. Some noises help to reinforce identity by linking fans with their favorite performers." What that young man in Central Park was listening to was

> little more than a hypnotic beat, a rythmic hammering to over-

> whelm all other sound and rock the submissive mind into a stupor. In these days of multiple frustrations, such noise can prove addictive, a drug to ease the pain of boredom of living. . . . People find silence unbearable, or indeed frightening. Two city youths in a tent on a Hebridean Island [in Scotland] came knocking at midnight, unable to bear the strain of lying listening to a silence broken by small sounds of mice or birds. Perception can be sharpened alarmingly in silence.
>
> *(Anthony Ross, "Elected Silence,"*
> The Tablet, *July 18, 1981)*

Perception can be sharpened alarmingly in silence.

Which brings me to the subject of retreats, about which I feel the need to say several things. Not so many of our people know about retreats, and I think the time has come when a few plain words for Episcopalians might be in order to allay suspicions, to settle prejudices, to realign perspectives, and generally to encourage a very good thing in the life of any soul that says it wants to love God.

First, we have good scriptural warrant for it. We really know very little about Christ's private life, but we know that his prayer-life with the Father was rich and constant. He was always at it. He prayed when others slept. Much of what he said was private, unknown, a secret between them both. Some of the things he said we know. He must have told somebody and it could have been John, the apostle he loved closely, probably because he was very young. John, you remember, was leaning or reclining next to Jesus at the Last Supper and heard his whispered asides. John recorded the majestic High Priestly Prayer in chapter 17 of his Gospel, uttered at that very time. It is long, mysterious, and deeply moving. We call it the High Priestly Prayer of Christ, interceding with the Father for the world. And he taught his disciples to pray. They asked him to teach them. He taught them words to say, words we say, the prayer called by the church the Lord's Prayer. And he taught them how to pray. The *how* is what concerns us. "'Come with me, by yourselves, to some lonely place where you can rest quietly.' (For they had no leisure even to eat, so many were coming and going)" (Mark 6:31). They did so: "they set off privately by boat for a lonely place"

(v. 32). Christ knew *from his own experience* that withdrawal, silence, solitude are very necessary.

Do not confuse this with the loneliness of being alone. That is hard to bear for some who live alone, who would love some human companionship, the sound of another voice, and to be loved and noticed by someone else. He wanted them to have not merely time to think, but a place to think and pray in, undistracted for a while. This is not selfish, this is not an evasion of responsibility to the clamant needs and necessities of those dependent on us. It is absolutely vital for balance, for bearing, for perspective, for planning, for prayer-life and for the soul's true peace. "Busyness" plays the very devil with our perspective and we shall never be the sort of priests and people we all ought to be until we realize that there is nothing cowardly or unreal in temporary withdrawal from involvement. Only so shall we learn that true involvement in the concerns and needs of others demands true depths of the spirit. We must wait still upon God before we plunge in. Otherwise our activity is often busybodying because our assessments are shallow. Christ spots this happening to his disciples, who have no leisure even to eat. Not only would people not leave them alone, they were possibly as much to blame by talking all the time. "No leisure even to eat." "*Vacate Deo,*" said St. Augustine, who knew all about this kind of thing, "Take a vacation toward God." Rest in the Lord.

A retreat is a miniature vacation toward God, for God is perfect rest as he is the perfection of all else. You remember the verse in the Psalm:

> *God is King, be the people never so impatient*
> *He sitteth between the cherubim, be the earth never so unquiet.*

Note that he sitteth to rule. He is at peace, at rest, even as he reigns in might over us. And he can do this because he is utterly at one with himself, and would like us to be. It is from the rest, the relaxation, the emptying of all unnecessary activity, that the activities of love, of imagination, and of prayer all come. For when we stop moving, when we stop talking—and that is hard for some of us—when we stop trying to make ourselves understood with our preferences, our needs, our points of view, then we have a chance to *listen*. If we listen as we *rest*, then it will not be that anxious sort of listening when someone is late coming home, listening for the key to turn in the lock, but rather the trustful, happy listening we do when someone beloved is with us. Only so shall we have the opportunity to hear God in the silence.

You will stand a better chance if you try to avoid saying anything to anyone at all except to God during the services. Here is what some people think is the crunch. It may be a new experience for you, not to talk. But have you tried it, knowing that people next to you and around you in church are trying it, and perhaps for the first time in their lives are having a door of discovery opened? Obviously as one who has so often done it I am used to it, but I tell you there are times when I yearn for it as I do for nothing else; "Speak, Lord," I say in the words of Samuel, "for thy servant heareth" (1 Sam. 3:9). I can only do that if I take the advice of a priest friend of mine who told me to sit down and shut up.

That is fine. But what do I *do* on retreat? I cannot talk, at least on the best and most meaningful regimen of a retreat. I am supposed to "keep silence, yea even from good words though it were pain and grief to me." (That is from the Psalms, too. There is a disconcerting amount of advice about keeping one's mouth shut in the Bible. God obviously thinks that our tongues, if not disciplined, can do a lot of damage. "The chatter of fools sounds like thorns burning under a pot.") We hear addresses, one in the morning and one in the evening, from the retreat conductor, and it is well to make notes of what he or she says. Oh yes! Some women are experts in this field, and I only wish more women would help us with their spiritual insight. The notes may help us to reflect upon and to turn over the things said. They may hit a nail which brings other things unhurriedly to mind, perhaps as you walk or as you rest, or even as you read some interesting book. Avoid newspapers; stick to a good novel or some biography or some history, and apply your mind. Use a Bible, or a hymnal, or the Prayer Book. Use the Psalms, if it is poetry you want as you think about God and your part in his plan and scheme of things. For deep in the still river of a quiet retreat you may learn things about yourself and God, and it may well be that you will want to put something right with him. You may feel you need the services of a priest, for counsel or confession, or both. There, in the silence of waiting upon God, is the time of times to come to terms with the Lord's demands, and your own performance.

True it is that confession is good for the soul. Before anyone gets alarmed let me place what I have to say in a theological setting. You will remember how at the Last Supper our Lord took a towel and girded himself with it. He knelt at his disciples' feet and began one by one to wash them, until Peter in a fit of false humility stopped him, "I will never let you wash my feet." And Christ looked at him and said, "If I do not wash you, *you are not in fellowship with me*" (John 13:8).

There is something deeply troubling here about Peter's humility. The superficial test of our humility is being willing to serve. A far keener test is whether we are willing to let Christ serve us, washing us and making us clean again. *That* is how our confessions should be seen, private or made in the presence of another forgiven sinner with the authority of declaring Christ's forgiveness. I tell you this. Either way is good. Either way is indispensable. We have to do it if we mean business and the time of retreat is ideal, when we can prepare without distraction after recollecting without interruption. It can and has changed a life. "Be still and wait upon God" is the best piece of advice to a fevered, overwrought spirit, and the continued, disciplined, regular practice of it has helped souls to saintliness. Perhaps our whole church needs to adopt that trademark—Quiet-Flo—and really begin to practice what we preach!

O let me hear thee speaking
In accents clear and still,
Above the storms of passion,
The murmurs of self-will.
O speak to reassure me,
To hasten and control,
O speak, and make me listen,
Thou Guardian of my soul.

Angels Unawares

HOW do you react when you are surprised? People will tell you that what you do in a moment of surprise will reveal a great deal about you. For you are at your most vulnerable point. Your defenses are down. You may lose your cool, as we say here in these United States. On the other hand, your real self may appear and its appearance may reassure your friends. God uses surprise as a means of making himself known to you—and to others.

In the late eighteen hundreds and well into this century, there was a saint of a man called Edward King. He was an Anglican priest who worked in a village parish close to Oxford. One very dark night, he was returning from seeing a poor old woman who was sick. That country lane hid a robber who later told this story. He was waiting to jump the lone traveler and to mug him, whoever he was. As he waited, he saw not one but two people approach him, the silent companion curiously bright with light which shone from within him and around him. That robber swore he had seen an angel companion alongside the unsuspecting Edward King, later to be known in our calendar as the Blessed Bishop Edward King of Lincoln. The surprise caught the robber at his most vulnerable moment. He was afraid, and Edward unknowingly walked past, free. Like Jacob on his journey from Beersheba to Haran. Do you remember this story? It's from Genesis 28:

> And he lighted upon a certain place, and tarried there all night, because the sun was set; and he took of the stones of that place, and put them for his pillows, and lay down in that place to sleep. And he dreamed, and behold a ladder set up on the earth,

> and the top of it reached to heaven: and behold the angels of God ascending and descending on it. And, behold, the Lord stood above it. . . . And Jacob awaked out of his sleep, and he said, Surely the Lord is in this place; and I knew it not. And he was afraid, and said, How dreadful is this place! this is none other but the house of God, and this is the gate of heaven.
>
> *(Vv. 11-17, KJV)*

Now, what happened in his surprise? He was afraid, vulnerable to terror at the surprise discovery he had made, for he realized he had been allowed to come very close to a glimpse of the hidden God. Not once, but twice. The other time was while he was very much alone, with a lot on his conscience (having cheated his brother from his rightful inheritance). In the night an angel of God challenged him to a wrestling match which lasted the night long and only ended after the angel had made a dirty throw and put Jacob's thigh out of joint. Jacob won the match. The Scriptures say, "he prevailed," and the realization came to him suddenly as he limped off into the early dawn that he had "seen God face to face." Once again, he was vulnerable to terror at the surprise discovery he had made, for he had been allowed, all unsuspectingly, to come very close to a glimpse of the hidden God.

God has, you see, a capacity for surprise in his dealings with us. And the agents he employs for his surprise confrontations and our surprise discoveries of him are what Holy Scripture describes as angels, messengers, heralds of his approach, ministering spirits. Before we dismiss them as fanciful, we would do well to remember that our Lord sanctions the mention of them in his teaching and very often refers to them. You have only to read St. Luke's account of our Savior's birth to see that angelic intervention is mentioned at every turn—and always, always, with the element of surprise. Luke often employs an adverb to describe their approach into the lives of the people with whom God makes a surprise intervention: "suddenly." Read the Gospel and you will see what I mean. An angel suddenly appears to the old priest called Zacharias. His aged and barren wife, Elizabeth, discovers that she is to have a child—who will become John the Baptist, the kinsman and forerunner of the Christ. An angel suddenly appears to Mary, who discovers that she is to bear God's son. Angels suddenly surround shepherds watching their flock and tell them of the Savior's birth. And with all these, as with Jacob and Edward King's assailant, their reaction is the same: terror or apprehension as the realization dawns upon them that God is making himself known, the God who hides himself only to make himself known, the God who hides himself to avoid being misunderstood, the God whose ways are not our ways, nor his thoughts our thoughts, and yet who longs for our eyes to light up in recognition of him and uses every way and means to make himself known. And as a means, he will use one of his angels.

Year by year the church rejoices in what we call the Solemnity of the Feast of St. Michael and All Angels. And each year the passages of Scripture read at Michaelmas bring us face to face with God's capacity for surprise as he uses angels as the means for making himself known.

Our reaction to these surprises can tell us not merely what we are like but where our faith is. I remember a spy story where a priest was making the sign of the cross over himself at some untoward happening, and an observer spotted that he did it not as a priest of the Western tradition, but from the Eastern tradition, which led to his exposure as a Communist spy. Of all the surprises in the world, a sudden death of someone we love can show where our faith is. Seemingly strong people who have been content to lead in a community of faith have lost that faith, and withdrawn from that community. This happened when the Angel of Death visited the child of someone I know. What a tragedy—this young life extinguished in terrible circumstances. In its suddenness, it overwhelmed my friend, and that friend has changed. Just slightly, but perceptibly, to those who know. But, again, I have seen a fresh determination and a deeper faith emerge, to build on what had been planted, for that loved one's sake. I have seen that sudden earthly separation trigger a person's consciousness to needs ignored before in the happiness once shared, and a concentration begun on a work to honor the beloved, as though in a mysterious way one were traveling lighter in the pursuit of that quest.

It may help us who are rightly and honestly incredulous to come to terms with the fact that there is a realm of the unseen, the invisible, the mysterious, to which there are no beaten paths of ecclesiastical history, no dates, no personal road signs of memory or anecdote or account. This feast makes us ponder that realm.

Before we are certain there are no such things as angels, let us examine our own grounds of certainty about things. There is the certainty born of prejudice which can land us as well as the object of our prejudice in uncomfortable situations. And when we air our prejudices, we deserve to be thought the fools we are. Nathanael could look down his nose and snort "Can any good thing come out of Nazareth?" certain that nothing could—and Jesus did. There are some good souls who can harbor a prejudice against the possibility of angels' existence because intellectually they want their faith as tidy as it can be. Angels are not a tidy addition. For some people the concept of intermediate spirits poses a threat to the Protestant concept that there shall be nothing between the soul and its Savior. So they are firm and certain in dismissing them from the scheme of things.

Second, there is the certainty born of ignorance. I confess I share your irritation and impatience at being on occasion obliged to listen to somebody who is a mine of misinformation blandly delivering himself of wrong facts. We can be very sure and very certain about things we know little of! Never having seen an angel, they say, they see no necessity for thinking there could be any. It brings back echoes of someone we love whose certainty matched his ignorance: "Unless *I see* the mark of nails on his hands, unless I put my finger into the place where the nails were, and my hand into his side, I will not believe it" (John 20:25). St. Thomas again! He must have been a great bore to the other disciples whose spiritual awareness as well as their shared experience had persuaded them that Christ was "risen from the dead and become the first fruits of them that slept." But he was spiritually unaware and obtuse in his unknowing. To him the words came from the resurrected Lord, "Be unbelieving no longer, but believe" (John 20:27).

Third, there is such a thing as the certainty born of disobedience, where the will rebels and hardens the mind to the contrary of the reasonable, the right, and the true. So you get the bigot. And bigotry can be pretty unattractive, trampling as it affirms and crushing where it tramples. Sometimes when we are less, rather than more, our true selves, our certainties can be a mixture of a couple of these ingredients. Enough said.

Finally, there is the certainty born of faith in and hope in and love for Christ himself, the certainty which comes from a willing surrender to God's will for us and for our lives; a sensitive, joyful, humorous attitude of the heart, the "ready heart" about which I find myself preaching so often. Such an attitude always is willingly vulnerable to the things that come along which bid fair to shake our faith. I'm not pleading for certainty in the existence of angels so much as pleading that we should be aware of the components of certainty and approach the realm of the invisible with Alice Meynell's hospitality of heart:

O be prepared, my soul!
To read the inconceivable, to scan
The myriad forms of God.

To a New Priest—The Ordinary and the Extraordinary

IT was a Hindu professor and diplomat at Oxford, Sarvarpelli Rhadakrishnan, who gave as his judgment that Christians are a bunch of very ordinary people making extraordinary claims. In two senses that hypercritical old academic was probably right. What I suspect first is that he was making a pejorative statement: there is little, if anything, to substantiate those extraordinary claims when you look at the lives of those who profess them; they were unchanged, uninspired, *un*different from the lives of people who didn't make those claims. They were unaffected by what they said they worshiped. And the Hindu simply could not come to terms with that. The lives of the people who shared his religious beliefs were profoundly affected by them. They were distinctive. They could not help being distinctive. The Christians he diagnosed had probably invented the chameleon: taking the exact colors and sometimes the texture of their surroundings and habitat and life.

He was probably right in a second sense, though he didn't know it. Christians have to be both ordinary *and* extraordinary. They have to be *in* the world as well as not of it. They cannot pretend that the world matters somewhat less in the scale of things heavenly. If they show less patience for it, less reverence for it, if they love *less* the things they see, how can they love things invisible? If they scorn it, they forget who made it, whose fingerprints are discernible at every turn, whose fragrance fills it, and whose voice can still be heard in it—the Divine Creator's. The Holy Spirit, the Divine Breath, makes her presence felt everywhere.

Do you know this?

The world is charged with the grandeur of God.
It will flame out, like shining from shook foil;
It gathers to a greatness, like the ooze of oil
Crushed. Why do men then now not reck his rod?

Generations have trod, have trod, have trod;
And all is seared with trade; bleared, smeared with toil;
And wears man's smudge and shares man's smell: the soil
Is bare now, nor can foot feel, being shod.

And for all this, nature is never spent;
There lives the dearest freshness deep down things;
And though the last lights of the black West went
Oh, morning, at the brown brink eastward, springs—
Because the Holy Ghost over the bent
World broods with warm breast and with ah! bright wings.

Gerard Manley Hopkins

The reality of that has to be continually rendered self-evident: otherwise, Christians will be so heavenly minded that they will be of no earthly use. Our place on God's earth is not a piece of divine absentmindedness. We are *meant* to be here.

That being so, Christians have to be ordinary *and* extraordinary. They are here to "maintain the fabric of the earth, and in their craft is their prayer" as the Scriptures say. And at the same time the call is for their lives to be "hid with Christ in God" as priests, for God's people are all priests, whether ordained or lay.

Both these things. This constant interplay and movement between the visible and the invisible; between the legitimate demands of this life and the life eternal; between the wisdom of this world *and* its relationship to the Divine wisdom and will; the priorities of this world, with those of heavenly things in mind; the reverence for life and the determination to protect it, and the Christian hope as we see it realized in the Sacraments—Jacob spotted this ceaseless traffic in his dream of the angels. I am reminded of this truth whenever I spend time in my vacation home in Bath where the ancient abbey has carved on its west wall the ladders up and down which angels go from earth to heaven and heaven to earth, and my sympathies are very much with one particular angel who, like myself, has vertigo and is looking anxiously over its shoulder, preferring earth to heaven perhaps, and certainly not relishing the journey.

The job of priesthood is all this: among lives both ordinary and extraordinary—among those whom St. Augustine once advised that a Christian has two eyes: one leveled at heaven and one on the earth, both to be open and alert—the job of priesthood is to make God's reality evident among our ordinariness. And that reality can be conveyed only if it has been glimpsed by the priest. The priest must have a firsthand tale to tell. Your access to it and your genuine familiarity with it are the things that make you priestly. But as with anything concerning God, there is a risk a priest has to take. Throughout history the term *priesthood* has been used with contempt for *not* being involved—certainly not wanting to be involved to the extent of getting its fingernails dirty—with the grit and the grime and the sweat and the semen of human encounter and endeavor, achievement and loss. It is a term used of a character who seeks refuge in a hidden authority to bolster his own, to bestow elusive prestige, and to win an argument when intellectually he can't win it, by claiming Divine inspiration for views held, allegations made, theories asserted, and prejudices cherished. It is a term used contemptuously for someone unsexed, both socially and biologically. It has many attitudes of unattractiveness, employed sneeringly like this.

But priesthood at work sacrificially and honestly is ravishingly, refreshingly different from what its detractors portray. Somehow or other a soul has come to terms with and has accepted a burden, a yoke, the added dimension of responsibility for the humanity it finds itself among. This strangely positioned commitment to people is not so much to improve their self-esteem, make them feel better about themselves, instruct them in self-improvement, mold them, or manage them, so much as to be among them with ease and naturalness and from the posture of being among them, to point to the traces of the God who hides himself, the clues to his mighty acts of redemption among us, the evidences of resurrection-life lived, and joy being discovered in all sorts of unlikely places. This pointing will obviously take the form of preaching and teaching, counseling and consoling. But no priest can point unless he has traveled the territory first, *has been there* to gain even a little first-hand experience of it, *some* familiarity with it, and personal commitment to the person and work of Christ whose country it is, and whose priestly obedience to his Father's will opened unto us the gate of everlasting life.

Preaching, yes; teaching, yes. But praying always through Christ to the Father in the power of the Holy Spirit, and never-endingly going into and coming from the presence of God with his people; needs and causes engraved on his hands and heart as he offers with Christ the sacrifice to the Father.

So the newly ordained priest must begin as he must continue: looking to Christ the Great High Priest standing in his vestments, with the whole world of you and me in his hands, on this, the Solemnity of his Exaltation into heaven. God's word has this to say to that priest: "Behold, I have engraven you upon the palms of my hands." Christ commits himself and his priesthood to his priests for time and for eternity. Our priesthood is part of his: we are engraven on his hands. When we receive the oil of anointing on our hands, we can say those words back to him. We can be a little Christ in the world he loves, totally at one with the people he has always loved and who surround us. We must look into their eyes as we pursue our priestly tasks and see him in them, looking at us. We might say this phrase silently as we meet them, greet them, work for them, deal with them, attempt to heal them, strive to strengthen them; only so shall we be the channel and vessel for his life to flood into theirs, so that they may live more abundantly and that their joy may be full. The ordinary and the extraordinary, bound together forever.

Singing the Lord's Song in a Strange Land

INDICATIONS are the Ecclesia Anglicana may be in danger of losing her nerve. Her prelates embarrass the faithful, pondering over credal matters in public as if their hearers were in a theological faculty classroom. Polarities exist about women and priesthood. Church membership has declined. So has her influence in this country.

Still, there is reason to sing. Something members and non-members cannot deny is the continuing vigor of the church's musical life and heritage. She takes music seriously. She has for over four hundred years. Every one of those centuries has produced jewels to be treasured—souls who have composed songs which have been sung, enriching the liturgies and offices. These continue to shine brightly in the light of common day.

Today we are beset with musical mediocrity in churches which have produced fine music in previous centuries. My concern, shared by many people around me who care, is that Anglican church music should lead the way in integrity, imaginativeness, and inspiration—for the congregations who sing it, and for the choirs who lead the congregations.

We ought to be proud of this contribution. Call it a civilizing influence in the life of the whole church which feels the agony of the poor, underprivileged, and oppressed, spending hours and days doing what it can to bring hope, alleviate injustice, and inculcate a sense of purpose to the lost.

Nevertheless, the church realizes that humankind's paramount activity is the worship of God. If she forgets this she is in trouble for sure. Using the ears and the voice in that worship is vital. Joining in song unites and is indispensable, strengthening the soul to meet the challenge human need presents outside the church doors.

We can learn much from the imaginative secular masters in our generation. In our eagerness to explore, we do well to remember that church music has to mind the demands and constraints upon it which carefully planned worship should make.

Music is the handmaiden of liturgy. Thus, there is little merit in music which makes congregations, choirs, or clergy self-conscious, or distracted, or contemptuous. Self-conscious worship is a curse; no, an abomination to the Lord, before whom we should be "lost in wonder, love, and praise"—on this side of life's river as much as upon a further shore.

It isn't good enough to deal only in old currency, tradeable as it still is. New coinage has to be minted without old values being debased. Exploration is brave. Nevertheless, what I see and hear of much new music gives me hope that we shall be able to bring new things out of our treasures.

I ought to pay tribute, now, to a remarkable man. He has helped me to appreciate and to encourage new composers, in my role as parish priest. He is a composer himself—a superb musicologist, organist, master chorister. His name is Gerre Hancock. He was in the saddle before I came to St. Thomas on Fifth Avenue in 1972.

Gerre and I have been great friends and close collaborators, both deeply interested in the genius of Anglican psalm chants and aware of their extraordinary capacity to bring words alive and alight with fresh meaning. (You can imagine my pleasure during Pope John Paul's New York visit, watching him listening, enchanted, to a psalm in St. Patrick's Cathedral set to an Anglican chant and sung extraordinarily well.)

Gerre's hymn accompaniment is famous, as are his improvisations. It is not at all unusual for him to be visited by church musicians from the far corners of the world. His rapport with choristers is extraordinary; his partnership with his parish priest, in church liturgies, is looked upon by many as a role model for musicians and priests alike.

Which brings me to the question of choral leadership. The choir isn't there to silence a congregation into passive acquiescence. Or to impress. Choirs are there to help us by leading the way so that we can follow gladly—with energy and delight. We, who have thrilled to hear against our own singing a descant rising like a lark above us, will know something of that exhilaration which brings joy to our being together. We find ourselves wanting to do more, making something beautiful for God.

There are special places, not many, where a highly trained choir—perhaps from a choir school—can sing stupendous stuff. There is plenty of this in Anglicanism.

This extraordinary legacy can't disappear. I write as someone with what the old Prayer Book calls the "inestimable benefit" of the only resident choir school in the Episcopal Church. I am spoiled, perhaps worse than I know. Yet I only have to think back to Easter Day when nearly three thousand voices seized the tune of a great hymn and took us as one to heaven's gate. When the glory of it had died into silence, one could still feel the vibration of angels' wings.

Anglicanism at its best makes astonishingly adult demands on the individual. At the same time it helps the single soul to meet these demands in a glad and joyful response. Anglican music at its best is the same. It energizes the devotion of the *Plebs Sancta Dei*—the holy common people of God.

God Gets His Own Back

THERE is all the difference in the world between human and Divine vengeance. Ours is tainted with revenge—"an eye for an eye and a tooth for a tooth." If we can add something more severe for good measure the chances are that we will. The Divine vengeance is different. God's mercy *is* his vengeance. Do not ask me how, but that is what happens, and people who have loved God and have made a life study of his ways will all tell you that.

Supremely we see it at this time. The world has always been preoccupied with itself: loving itself, hating itself, tricking itself, vaunting itself, exploiting itself, with scarcely a thought for the heart of love which makes the world go 'round; hardly a remembrance of the generosity of the Life-Giver and Sustainer and the Source of all our wisdom and inventiveness. It has found itself fascinating and it is in one hell of a mess. Just that. One *hell* of a mess—a mess and a predicament without him, which is what hell can in the end mean.

God gets his own back at our selfish self-*in*sufficiency by bringing his vengeance not in a cataclysm, not in a calamity, but in a baby's cry. He himself suddenly is among us as we are, one of us, helpless and vulnerable like the least of us, poor like most of us, dependent on love like all of us. He places himself in our predicament, he gives himself to a world that has never dreamt he would do it and has never really wanted him among us. That is his vengeance. His vengeance is his mercy. He simply would not take no for an answer, and risks being unwanted, unrecognized, unwelcome, and generally in the way. Since we did not give ourselves in love to him, his vengeance has been that he has given himself to us. To do so, he courts disaster, he invites disagreement—yet he takes that risk. He comes, and he appears within a situation which is unfortunate, ill-timed so far as the world's inconvenience and comfort are concerned. We would put him off forever, if we could. He becomes the uninvited guest, the man who stayed to dinner and brought not respectability to the table, not good luck, or even conviviality. He brought food. Food for life eternal. Himself. He keeps on bringing himself to our table of discontent and disappointment, failure and foolishness, and he sweetens our diet and keeps us alive.

The secret is that his vengeance has succeeded. He has won. He has reclaimed us for himself, us whom he loves and gives life to. True it is then, in every meaning of the phrase, he *has got his own back.*

The Checkerboard: For Christmas

OUTSIDE interference is something none of us enjoys. We have our turf and we do not appreciate others on it. We know our worth and we do not appreciate others undervaluing it. We claim our prerogatives and it is no fun having others claiming theirs and infringing upon ours in the process. All of us, whether we are princes or prostitutes or ordinary private citizens, resent somebody on our "beat."

Humanity is just like that. We stake out our claims and if we can add a yard or two or an acre or two or a province or two or a nation or two, all the better. Self-aggrandizement and self-protection are the name of the game. We invented the game, but who owns the checkerboard we are playing on? We forget and we have always forgotten that it belongs to God. In our constant maneuverings, in our self-absorption with the game across the centuries and down the corridor of the ages we forget that we are watched, not from outside but from within the very game itself. And on one historic occasion the great and gentle hand of God introduces another player: himself, as one of us. We begin to notice that there is a difference in the game this new player employs. It is known by a four-letter word: love. His rules of the game are different and we resent that. He plays differently and it affects us all. We do not appreciate what we call this *outside interference* when in fact it is nothing of the kind. It is from the deepest recesses of the interior: from the heart of the living God himself. But we do not know who it is and we do not like the interference.

So Christ is born among us as we squabble and posture and strut upon the checkerboard. The sound of our assertions and claims almost deafens the world. But the cry of a baby is heard in the ears of simple folks to whom the first cry of a newborn lamb is a cause of joy and a call to duty—shepherds. They run, they see, they recognize God among us and the new game has begun in which meekness and obedience will win and "Divine weakness, stronger than man's strength," as the Scriptures say, will win in the end. For the tiny cry for love is itself the love stronger than death, which gives life and light and salvation to the world.

What We Owe to Bishop John Allin

THE Bible often mentions visions. Many of the prophets tell us what they have seen and what they have felt on seeing them. St. John on the Isle of Patmos, in exile there, saw a new Jerusalem, and he describes a restored and rejuvenated City of God, but a new city from which the blights upon the lives of its citizens have been forever banished: no more bereavement because no more death, no more pain, no more sense of loss and deprivation. John was presented with a vision of life in which God's life was victorious. There could be no more anxiety—there was no more sea, the sea representing the dark turbulence and chaos and formless threat to human life, the struggle inherent in shaping Creation. He saw life and all existence without guessing its uncertain futures and risking mistake in trying to discern its histories. The eternal was the present, for Christ had made all things new, and what he saw was God's own life in the splendor of its existence.

I love that passage of Scripture from the Book of Revelation, which God disclosed to John. He writes in poetry, in riddle, in a tumbled skein of colors and shapes, a sort of surrealist account. People have been quick to see their own interpretations emerge from this puzzling poetry, and the truth is that it *is* possible for different people to discover different colors in it as people can when they look at oil on water; they catch the refractions of the light.

It is a legitimate exercise for people to ponder the life and the doings of their God, to wait and look and look again and try to see the emergence of a shape they recognize, a form they can identify, from the mystery of his hiddenness. What does he have in store for the world of humanity, for me as an individual, for the church which Christ came to build, peopled as it is with stupid and sinful liars like myself, where saints are suspected for being different, and disregarded, where we can hardly ever see the wood for the trees, where we solemnly and pompously make pronouncements that are wrong, self-serving, and unintelligent? It is a world where we play God and judge where we have no right to judge, and where, but for the strong life of the risen Christ lived on in it, the whole shaky edifice most deservedly would have shattered and fallen forever.

I listen to this great vision and the picture of the church in its perfection, which after all is what heaven is—all Creation joined in the music of praise and love of its Divine Creator, undeterred, uninterrupted, unconstrained, as it gives back the song which now the angels sing—and I am inspired. With this vision of a reality too bright for me to contemplate for more than the blink of an eye, I feel more sanguine when I turn again to the things of earth, and when I look at that part of the church of God which holds my loyalty and my love, unsatisfactory as she allows herself to be viewed; flawed, stained, uncertain and weakened by the likes of me. I wonder about her immediate future.

She has made an important decision this year [1985], in this part of her. She has chosen a new chief shepherd who, if all goes as she plans, will be with us a number of years; and in a position to influence her shape, her priorities, her direction: our new Presiding Bishop. But first I think it is about time the Episcopal Church in the United States pulled itself together to consider the contribution of our Presiding Bishop John Allin. There has been, if I may say so, a singular, noticeable lack of reaction on the part of the church to the news of who the new Primate is, Edmund Browning. People had never particularly heard of him. That is understandable. I do not think it matters very much that he is an unknown quantity. Bishop John Allin was an equally unknown quantity as Bishop of Mississippi. Edmund Browning had been working quietly and faithfully as the Bishop of Hawaii, and he is not renowned for his scholarship or his preaching or his statesmanship or his leadership. He has been a faithful servant of his priests and people and he comes to his new task with no pretensions to greatness or grandeur of any sort. What the press have said he has said has not allayed some apprehensions I and others share about what bishops in general do and do not say. We can be forgiven for hoping that bishops will teach us about God. That means they must use Holy Scripture. The office of bishop in the church of God is a teaching office, directed to the flock of which he is the chief pastor and shepherd of the shepherds. So his teaching has two dimensions, two reaches. He is first directed to the clergy, themselves the teachers and guardians of the faith in the communities they serve, who are the encouragers and the enablers of the people of God who constitute the second dimension and reach of his teaching, for they themselves are the evangelists, the effective gospel-spreaders for Christ. Many priests would be grateful for this teaching and glad to pass the benefits of it to their people. A bishop's teaching is not necessarily to provide all the answers anyone may care to ask. But there are guidelines he must be mindful of, and some remarks from the present Archbishop of Canterbury, Robert Runcie, may well be heard at this point.

> If he is true to his vocation a bishop must regard himself as preeminently the trustee of tradition. . . . A bishop has, according to Church law, to "teach and uphold sound and wholesome doctrine, and to banish and drive away all erroneous and strange opinions." He . . . has a conservative responsibility. He is a guarantor of historic continuity. He is a steward of the Apostolic Faith.

Words of support for this come from no less a quarter than John Robinson, the onetime Bishop of Woolwich, who wrote the disturbing book *Honest to God:*

> A bishop will be the more aware that his slightest word is liable to be taken up and sometimes distorted by the public media. His utterances and actions will therefore appear, particularly outside the Church but also to embarrassed faithful within, to commit many others than himself. This means he must exercise special prudence and imagination.

Archbishop Runcie adds: "Churches are habitually engaged in

correcting their own past. But such change is done by emendation, by development, by reemphasis and not by repudiation."

Strong words, these. We can also say that once a bishop ventures into the area of a political party in commenting upon contemporary events he may alienate Christians within his own jurisdiction who see things in a different political light while holding firm to orthodox and traditional Christian articles of faith. When those areas deal with questions of social justice, people's poverty or unemployment, hopes for peace from nuclear warfare, birth control, abortion, or capital punishment, he finds he has a minefield to walk in, and folks are swift to leap to conclusions they think he has found and embraces. The press and media coverage can be less then helpful when they edit or highlight certain phrases and sentences in a statement he may have prepared with a balance in mind. If he is flippant or out for the telling phrase, he will get what he deserves. Where prudence gives way to courage, where the teacher becomes the statesman, where the shepherd reaches for the mantle of the prophet, we must always remember the whole of Christ's church, and the church contains the *least of these, Christ's brethren,* who may be slow of heart and mind and to whom damage takes the longest to heal. He has to be mindful of history as well as the future, the great church of St. John's vision as of the present predicament. And he has to lead. A shepherd leads. He does not prod or bark orders from the bridge. He leads his flock.

This I would ask you to consider in what the present Presiding Bishop John Allin has done. He came into his office in a church embittered with argument and strife, riddled by faction. The sickening sixties had played havoc with this nation and the church in all its parts within it. There was anger on a national scale, there was guilt over issues like the war in Vietnam. There was shame at its outcome. There was a series of looming financial crises. There was a discovering of ways of looking at God set against this social and economic turmoil which dismayed some people. Landmarks were torn up and cast away. Sometimes the new discoveries were hailed as new revelations. Theology and its study were jolted in the schools and seminaries. New forms of spirituality were explored and exploited, sometimes recklessly. People forget a lot, perhaps too much at times in their attempts to accommodate what they welcomed as the *new thing*.

But John Maury Allin had read his Scripture. The New Jerusalem, the church of heaven, was a vision to which its participants must arrive in peace, in deliberate and delicate approach, mindful of history, mindful of tradition, supremely mindful of reverence owed to the Divine Lord, courageous in trying new ways and patient to see their outcome.

He wanted to bring his people with him, bruises and all, at a pace which the wounded could manage. He urged integrity, truth, and charity, rather than vast expediency or slow caution. Of course he has been a traditionalist. Remember Robert Runcie's words of reminder on that. He has irked some. He has angered others. Examine their agendas before joining them.

He has brought with him a sweet reasonableness and reality of Fatherhood of a vast and unmanageable family. In so doing, he has taught us about God. And that is what bishops are for. A peacemaker rather than a pacemaker. A priest rather than a pragmatist, who has as St. Augustine enjoins us all to have: one eye on the things of heaven and one on the things of earth, and both open and alert.